Practical stage make-up

710021201-0

Philippe Perrottet

Practical stage make-up

Studio Vista

To my wife for her patience and encouragement

Studio Vista
Cassell and Collier Macmillan Publishers Ltd
35 Red Lion Square, London WC1R 4SG

ISBN 0 289 70496 0

Set in 11/12 Garamond
Made and printed in Great Britain by
The Camelot Press Ltd, Southampton

Contents

Acknowledgements

The author and publishers wish to thank the following for permission to reproduce their photographs: Max Factor Salon (Plates 1 & 22), Sadler's Wells (Plate 20), Reg Wilson (Plates 14 & 16), Houston Rogers (Plates 15 & 18), Donald Southern (Plates 19 & 21), Paul Hamlyn (Plates 23 & 24), Timothy O'Brien (Plates 45 & 46), and Angus McBean (for all remaining plates).

The author also wishes to thank Eve Gardiner and Douglas Young of the Max Factor Salon for practical assistance.

1 · What sort of make-up and why

A great amount of the make-up worn in both the professional and amateur theatre of today is applied without thought, and without any sound reason behind its structure or colour. Many performers, if asked why they wear a particular make-up (or indeed, why they wear make-up at all), are unable to give a reasonable answer. Many fall back on saying that they have copied what they have seen worn by other artists, or used a colour that has looked nice on another performer.

The main purpose of stage make-up is to make the performer's face look right (not necessarily natural) to the public in the context of the production and its design, and in the theatre in which it is being performed. From this it follows that a make-up which is suitable in one production, or in one theatre, may be quite wrong in another. Make-up can range from the grotesquely heavy to no make-up at all, and still be right for a certain production or theatre. The problem for the performer is to know what is correct for each set of conditions. A good director will usually indicate to a performer what is required, but not many directors have the technical knowledge to explain in detail how to achieve a desired effect.

Designers can always explain what sort of effect they want, but very rarely do they have any idea how the artist is to set about achieving it (some of the worst make-up that I have seen has been done by designers). It is a great help to the performers if there is someone to design the make-up and impose an overall style, and also to explain how to achieve the effect by simple means.

In many continental theatres there is a make-up artist, who attends to the make-up of all the performers, as in films and television in this country. This can be extremely successful, and can equally be rather dull – it depends entirely on the calibre of the make-up artist. When the Hamburg Opera visited Sadler's Wells Theatre in 1962, I was very impressed by the high standard of make-up, and by the way in which the faces were all made up in the same style – the result of all being done by the same first-class make-up artist.

The first thing to decide is the type of make-up at which one is aiming. Make-up falls into several groups, which may then be further sub-divided. These are 'straight', 'character', 'stylised' and 'fantastic' (these last two overlap considerably). The first speaks for itself. The aim is to make one's face look exactly the same, on the stage, in costume (and wig, if necessary) and under stage lighting, as it does in real life. The second covers a much larger field: making the face look older, fatter, thinner, changing the character of the face to appear villainous or angelic, or even changing the nationality or racial type (becoming Mediterranean, Asiatic, etc.). The third is dictated by the style of the production. If in a production of a Greek drama, for example, the costumes have been designed to look as if they have been hewn from stone, then a naturalistic face will look wrong. The face will need to look as if it has been hewn from stone as well. 'Fantastic' speaks for itself, and is more often met with in opera and ballet than in drama. The style depends entirely on the designer. If the performer is intended to look like a Russian wooden doll, or a Picasso painting, then his or her face must be painted to simulate a wooden doll or a Picasso painting. Fortunately, the details are usually shown on the costume design and can be copied or adapted to the face.

The next thing is to discover how effects are achieved with make-up. Many performers paint lines and shadows on to their faces with no clear idea of what they are trying to achieve – they have just seen other performers doing the same thing. Used properly, every line and detail of a make-up has a sound structural reason behind it. The main purpose of 'straight' make-up is to adjust the colour of the face to the stage lighting, to counteract any lack of balance caused by the angle or direction of the lighting (make-up still suffers from many things intended to counteract the effect of strong footlights, which are rarely used nowadays), and to enlarge or exaggerate details which do not carry at a distance.

The general effect of distance and strong lighting is to eliminate detail and fade colours. To counteract the effects of this, faces are painted in a stronger colour, and details such as eyes, eyebrows and mouths are quite heavily accentuated. Naturally, in a theatre the size of the Royal Opera House, Covent Garden, or the Metropolitan Opera House in New York, the distances are much greater and the lighting is brighter, so a much heavier make-up is needed than in an intimate theatre such as the Arts Theatre, London, the Mayfair in New York, or a village hall. These, of course, are extremes and there are many graduations in between. There is, however, one comforting thought – a really well applied make-up adapts itself surprisingly. A lot of make-up in the right places usually looks better in a small theatre than a little badly applied, and vice versa.

This leads to another extraordinary fact. It is possible to break many of the generally accepted rules of make-up, and still look right – IF you know what you are doing. If the make-up looks right from the front, then it is right, no matter how it has been achieved. Equally, a well applied make-up in a wrong style, or in a style or colour different from the other faces on the stage, will look wrong. If a performer is the only one out of step, no matter how well applied his or her make-up is, it will look wrong to the audience.

Fashions in everyday make-up for women play a considerable part in stage make-up, in two ways: the more obvious is that if an actress is playing a fashionable woman on the stage, she will have to wear what appears to the audience as a fashionable make-up. The less obvious effect is in conditioning us to accept as natural things that are obviously artificial. For many years (or even decades), it has been normal to see women with their mouths painted in various bright shades of pink and red, and an actress with her mouth painted to look natural would give an effect of more than rustic simplicity. On the other hand, in some periods, we have become accustomed to seeing very pale pink and even white lips on some girls, and on a suitable stage character we would accept them as normal, as we also accept artificial eyelashes at present. There has also been at times an exaggerated form of eye make-up being worn for everyday which would pass as a straight make-up if worn on the stage. To convey the impression of a character wearing such a make-up, it would be necessary to exaggerate it even further for the stage.

Although these passing fashions in everyday make-up appear natural with contemporary dress, they rarely combine successfully with period costume. When *Count Ory* was first produced at Sadler's Wells, the prima donna wore her own pale pink lipstick, which exactly matched the colour of her (visible) petticoat. The effect was beautiful in the dressing room, but at the dress rehearsal a number of people asked me if she was made up to look ill! We eventually settled for a more traditional red, slightly softened to blend with the costume.

In the following chapters I shall describe the technique of applying a make-up, first in general, then in more detail. I have tried to explain the structural reasons for most things as I describe how to do them, and I also point out some of the more peculiar habits that remain in use for no real reason. Many, as mentioned before, are left over from old-fashioned lighting. Early electric stage lighting flattened the structure of the face, and it was necessary to counteract it with painted shadings and highlights. Lighting nowadays is nearly always directional, that is, shafts of light from various angles instead of an overall brilliance. This picks up the shape of the facial structure without needing additional assistance from make-up.

Several methods of applying make-up are described, using different types of make-up made by Max Factor and Leichner – these two makes are the most used, and are available in most parts of the world. I give the method that I use myself first, in each case, not because it is the best, but because I have always found it the most satisfactory. Other people find other ways better, or other kinds of make-up more suitable for their type of skin. Having spent most of my stage career as a dancer, I naturally use the quickest and easiest way to an objective. Dancers frequently have to change their entire make-up, as well as their costume, in a fifteen-minute interval. This makes them avoid unnecessary detail and eliminate anything that does not make its effect fully to the audience. Many people like to spend a great deal of time building up a make-up in tiny detail, but I have never worked in this way, and do not describe that method in this book.

Nowadays there are three main kinds of foundation or base used in general theatre make-up. These are cream (in two varieties: Max Factor Satin Smooth Panchromatic [my favourite, for reasons given in chapter 3] and Leichner Spotlite Klear); Leichner greasepaint, the traditional sticks of colour; and finally Max Factor Pancake and Panstik. Most performers use a rather free mixture of all these types, sometimes successfully, sometimes less so. In chapter 3 there is a description of how to do a complete straight make-up, using each of these bases in turn.

Finally, the only way to achieve a good make-up is by practice. Make yourself up, look to see what is wrong, and then start all over again, time after time. It is one thing to know what you want to achieve, and another actually to achieve it. Do not be discouraged if your first attempts look like Theda Bara in an early silent film. It is only practice that will make you able to achieve a good result. One must also bear in mind the truism that no two faces are alike; choose from the alternate techniques the one that seems most suitable, and then become adept at it. Once one has mastered a basic technique, then it can be extended to include all the categories of make-up.

2 · Equipment and materials ✓

It is not necessary for a performer to carry a complete stock of make-up in the hope that it will be needed sooner or later, but it is surprising how many people have make-up boxes crammed with sticks and tubes that have never been used. If one starts with the things that are actually used in a straight make-up, and then adds extra items as they are required, a great deal of unnecessary expense and clutter can be avoided.

The basic requirements for the different types of foundation are given here in separate lists, and the general make-up required for all the rest of the make-up (eye lining, shading, etc.) is listed after them. There are charts giving the suggested colours for Max Factor Satin Smooth, Pancake and Panstik. Like all make-up, these vary slightly on different skins so it is impossible to be dogmatic about colours, but those listed should be reasonably suitable under most conditions. The lower numbers are always the paler shades, so a performer of medium dark colouring should choose the paler shade under the dark listing, and so on. There are no charts for Leichner greasepaints, as foundations from these are blended with several sticks which are indicated in the greasepaint foundation section, nor is there one for Leichner Spotlite Klear. These are based on the greasepaint colours, and I consider them better blended than used straight. However, Peach can be used alone as a pale pink foundation, Dark Peach as a strong pink, Peach Special as a hot pink tan and Lit K as a strong, rather orange tan. With greasepaint or Spotlite Klear, Leichner Neutral blending powder can be used for pale foundations, and Brownish blending powder for darker ones.

Foundation with Max Factor Satin Smooth

> One tube of basic colour (see chart p 12)
> One box of powder (Translucent (c3–238))
> One stick Leichner No. 9 (women) *or* No. 8 (men)

Foundation with Max Factor Pancake

> One cake of basic colour (see chart p 12)
> One cake of dry rouge: Technicolour for women
> > > Dark Technicolour for men

Foundation with Max Factor Panstik

> One stick of basic colour (see chart p 12)
> One cake dry rouge (as with Pancake)
> One box powder (Translucent (c3–238))

Foundation with Leichner Spotlite Klear

> One tube basic colour (see p 14)
> *or* Two tubes for blending (see chapter 3)
> One stick No. 9 Leichner greasepaint (women) *or* No. 8 (men)
> One tin powder (see above)

Foundation with Leichner greasepaint

> WOMEN One stick No. 5
> One stick No. 9
> *possibly* One stick Lit K (see chapter 3)
> *possibly* One stick No. 6 (see chapter 3)
> One tin powder (see above)

MEN   One stick No. 5
       One stick No. 8
possibly One stick Lit K (see chapter 3)
possibly One stick No. 4½ (see chapter 3)
       One tin powder (brownish)

Armed with one of these basic foundations, one can continue to complete the collection of make-up.

For eye lining one requires

       One black or brown eyebrow pencil (see chart p 12)
or   One brush (No. 3 sable watercolour, or eye lining brush)
with One stick black or brown Leichner greasepaint (see chart p 12)
or   Max Factor black or brown eye lining (see chart p 12)
or   A proprietary liquid black or brown eye liner (see chart p 12)
       (If either of these two last are used, then a black or brown eyebrow pencil or black or brown greasepaint is required for the eyebrows.)
       One bundle orange-sticks (small manicure sticks)
       Black or brown mascara (to match eye lining)
       One Leichner dark blue liner, No. 326
or   A suitable colour eyeshadow (see chapter 3)
       One Leichner white liner (No. 22) for large theatres

For lips, cheeks, etc., with cream and grease foundations

       One stick of Leichner carmine 2
       One stick of Leichner carmine 3
       (Performers using a Pancake foundation may use these with either Leichner No. 8 or No. 9 for their lips, or they can use Max Factor moist rouge in a colour to match their cheek colour.)

For highlighting with cream and grease foundations

       One stick Leichner No. 5 greasepaint

For general use

       One large velour powder puff
       One small mirror on a stand
       One large roll cotton wool
or   One large packet tissues
       One tin removing cream
or   One bottle medicinal liquid paraffin
or   One bottle olive oil

This is all that is required for a straight make-up, with the exception of a box to keep it in.

For corrective shading one requires

       One stick Leichner No. 3 green greasepaint
or   One cake suitable coloured Pancake (see chapter 6)

For character make-up one also requires

For cream or grease foundations

       One Leichner lake liner (No. 25)
       One Leichner dark brown liner (No. 28)

SUITABLE COLOURS IN MAX FACTOR SATIN SMOOTH OR PANSTIK				
	Straight Plays	Musicals, Opera and Ballet	Powder	Eye Lining
FAIR WOMEN	24	24 or 25	Trans (C3–238)	Brownish/Black or Black (M.O.B.)
DARK WOMEN	25	25 or 26	,,	Black
FAIR MEN	27	28 or 29	,,	Brownish/Black or Black (M.O.B.)
DARK MEN	29	29 or 30	,,	Black

SUITABLE COLOURS IN MAX FACTOR PANCAKE OR PANSTIK				
FAIR WOMEN	23 or CTV.3W	23 or Straight Female	No powder is needed with Pancake. With Panstik use Trans. (C3–238)	Brownish/Black or Black (M.O.B.)
DARK WOMEN	25 or CTV.5W	25 or Straight Female		Black
FAIR MEN	Natural Tan or CTV.9W	Beige Tan or 27		Brownish/Black or Black (M.O.B.)
DARK MEN	Beige Tan or Light Egyptian	29 or Latin		Black

(M.O.B.) means musicals, operas and ballet
Translucent (C3–238) powder can be worn over make-up of any colour from palest pink to Negro, without affecting the original colour of the base.

For Pancake and Panstik foundations
One Box Shading (734) Max Factor Lining Colour (warm shading)
One Box Shading (1363) Max Factor Lining Colour (paler shading)
One Box White (12) Max Factor Lining Colour (highlighting)
One tin talc

With a full set from this for the type of foundation required, there is very little that cannot be achieved. When one is wearing a special make-up for a short period, a colour can be made up from the materials at hand, except with Pancake, which does not blend and must always be bought in the colour required. If the make-up is needed for a long run, it is better to buy a suitable coloured foundation from the large range available. Pancake colours are suggested for the various effects discussed throughout the book, and many of the same colours are available in Panstick and Satin Smooth. These may be added to the make-up box as they are needed, as may additional colours in Leichner greasepaint.

Men with reddish-blonde hair often have trouble in achieving a natural colour with Pancake, as something in the pigmentation of their skin turns most Pancakes a bright orange. I have known two performers share the same cake of Pancake, and whereas one was the correct colour, the other (who was of this type) was intensely orange. This trouble can be overcome by using Pancake Natural tan K.F.7, which does not change its colour when applied to this type of skin.

3 · Basic facial make-up

We can assume that the make-up is being done in normal dressing room conditions, in front of a standard make-up table. This usually consists of a shelf about eighteen inches deep, attached to the wall, with a mirror fixed to the wall behind it, and lit by lights either around or above the mirror. The make-up base, shading and powder are usually applied looking into the fixed mirror, and for the eye and eyebrow make-up and highlighting a small hand mirror is used, so that the detail can be seen at close range.

When practising make-up away from the theatre, it is advisable to approximate dressing-room conditions as closely as possible, as the lighting and distance from the mirror can strongly affect the finished effect. A board placed over a washbasin that has a mirror behind it with an overhead light is perhaps the best substitute for a proper theatre dressing table.

Preparing the face

Make-up, not surprisingly, goes best on a clean face, with no previous make-up, sweat or grime on it. After the face has been washed, it is advisable to have a cold rinse, or to use an astringent or skin freshener to close the pores. Make sure that you are not wearing any clothes that have to be taken off over your head, as they can take the make-up with them. The best thing to wear is an old dressing gown (it is bound to get some make-up on it). An old towel laid over your knees will catch loose powder, and you will need an even older towel or some tissues to wipe your fingers clean as you progress. Many women wear a make-up band or a bandage to keep make-up and powder out of their hair.

The foundation, with Max Factor Satin Smooth Panchromatic

This is the foundation that I find most practical. It has the advantage of being a fixed colour (a great help when making up in inadequate lighting) and at the same time one can easily blend in other colours or shadings.

Squeeze a little (about a quarter of an inch) out of the tube, and dab it in little dots all over the face and under the chin. Then, with the fingers of both hands, rub it evenly all over the face and halfway down the neck. The colour should be spread as thinly as possible – it should be stretched over the face. If there is a greasy patch anywhere, wipe it off with a tissue or some cotton wool and then smooth over again with your fingers. The result should be a fairly matt, completely even colour from the hairline (but not rubbed into the hair) to halfway down the neck, where it fades into the natural skin colour – take care not to leave a hard line. When a high collar is being worn in the performance, then the make-up is not taken so far down; and conversely, with a low neckline, the make-up is taken down to the base of the neck and faded out there. With low-cut dresses a body make-up is usually worn (see chapter 17). The ears should be lightly brushed over with the fingers while they have make-up on them. Do not try to make them up in detail – the result is not sufficient to justify the trouble.

Wipe the hands clean and take a stick of Leichner No. 9 (women) or No. 8 (men). Rub a little on the second finger of the right hand, and spread it along under each eyebrow and slightly over the outside end of the eyebrow (FIG I). Wipe the finger clean, and then spread the colour down and fade it out towards the eye socket.

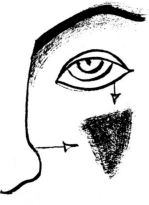

FIG I

13

Put a little more 8 or 9 on the same finger, and shade in a shield shape on each cheek, the centre being below the outside half of the eye, and in a straight line horizontally with the top of the nostrils (FIG 1). The exact placing varies slightly with each face, and it may take a little experimenting. Fade the edge of the colour into the foundation with a clean finger, so that the change of colour is reasonably imperceptible. Women may then add a dot of Leichner carmine 2 or 3 to the centre of the patch of colour, and fade it in, in the same way. Do not place the cheek colour beside the eyes or up on the temple – this is a style of make-up dating from the time of gas-lit stages, and looks completely unnatural on any reasonably lit stage.

If corrective shading (discussed in chapter 6) is being used, it is applied now.

It is now time to powder, using the appropriate coloured powder from the chart. A powder that does not match can completely alter the colour of the make-up, especially when lit by a strong cross light. Dip your puff (which should be of the large velour type) firmly into the powder, and press it evenly all over the face, down over the neck to slightly below where the foundation finishes, and over both ears. When the powder has been pressed in evenly all over the face the result should resemble a ghost. Take the puff, or a piece of cotton wool, and lightly dust off all the surplus powder. You should now have a fairly brightly coloured matt surface, with slightly brighter colour showing on the cheeks and under the eyebrows.

The foundation, with Leichner Spotlite Klear ✓

This is used in exactly the same way as Satin Smooth if there is a colour that suits your requirements. The best effects are achieved by blending two colours, using those suggested in the section on greasepaint foundations (the colours are the same and have the same numbers). Dab the two colours over the face, and then proceed in the same way as with Satin Smooth. If using the named shades referred to in chapter 2, p 10, try a little on your hand when selecting the colour, as some of them may appear much more pink in use than in the tube.

The foundation, with Leichner greasepaint ✓

This is the traditional form of make-up and some performers prefer it as being the most flexible, because it is possible to blend the various sticks to many different shades. It has the corresponding disadvantage that, as it is a blend, it is necessary to judge the correct colour for every performance. When touring and using different dressing-room conditions every week, this can call for a good deal of experience and judgement.

The traditional colours are Nos. 5 and 9 for both men and women. I consider this is suitable for fairer women who want a rather pink make-up. For brunettes, a combination of Lit K and No. 6 gives a warm tan which is more acceptable. A creamier tan can be made with Lit K and No. 5. For men, Nos. 5 and 8 give a rather florid complexion which is improved by the addition of a little Lit K, and a more natural effect can be achieved with Lit K and No. 4½. The proportions can only be ascertained by experiment. I do not consider No. 9 a suitable colour for men, as it gives too pink a tone to the face. One must be careful not to use too much of the darker colours (Nos. 8 and 9), or the resulting colour will be too florid.

Take a stick of the basic colour that you are using (No. 5 or Lit K) and draw four good stripes of colour across the forehead and down both cheeks, and two stripes down the sides of the nose. Then take the darker colour (Nos. 8, 9, etc.) and draw two stripes between those already drawn (one down the centre of the nose). Using the fingers of both hands spread the greasepaint over the face, blending the colours until an even texture and colour is obtained from the hairline (but not rubbed into the roots of the hair) to halfway down the neck, where it fades into the natural colour. This should be adjusted to suit the costume. If a low neckline is being worn, the colour should continue to the base of the neck, and with a very low neckline, body make-up should be worn (see chapter 17). The ears should be lightly brushed over with the fingers while they have make-up on them. Check the colour, and if necessary adjust it by adding more of the darker or lighter shade. Additional colour should be added in small dots all over the face, which makes it easier to work in evenly. When the correct colour is achieved, bearing in mind that it must be considerably stronger than the natural colour, to allow for the effects of lighting and distance, proceed as described in the third paragraph of the section on foundation with Max Factor Satin Smooth.

The foundation with Max Factor Pancake or Panstik ✓

Pancake is undoubtedly the quickest and easiest form of foundation, and this automatically makes it also the most abused. Performers frequently apply a hurried, thick coating of an inappropriate colour with the result that from the audience they appear to have a face coated with yellow mud. Panstik is also apt to be abused, usually by being applied too thickly. Properly used, both these can be extremely effective foundations, each with its own special advantages: Pancake has an ability to blot out structural detail, which is very useful for Oriental make-up, and for making an older face appear young. Panstik, properly used, gives the lightest and most natural of all foundations. Both are very suitable for intimate theatres and cabaret.

Both foundations are applied with a wet sponge, and both should be applied as lightly as possible.

Use a cosmetic sponge (Max Factor make them in two suitable sizes) to apply the Pancake or Panstik, wetting it thoroughly and then squeezing out the bulk of the water. Wipe the damp sponge over the Pancake or Panstik and lightly spread the colour over the face and halfway down the neck, fading it out gently. Wipe the sponge lightly over the ears. You should then have an even, matt colour over the entire face, from the hairline to halfway down the neck. If a low neckline is being worn the colour should continue to the base of the neck, and with an extremely low neckline, body make-up should be worn (see chapter 17).

Now apply a dab of Max Factor dry rouge to the centre of each cheek, with the small pad provided. Use Technicolour for women, and Dark Technicolour for men (for very brightly coloured cheeks, women can use Blondeen – as the name suggests, it is more suitable for blondes). The dabs of colour should be about three-quarters of an inch across, and should be below the outside half of the eye and in a straight line horizontally with the top of the nostril (FIG 1). Blend these in with a sponge lightly charged with the same Pancake or Panstik that was used for the foundation. The final shape of the cheek colour should be a cross between a shield and a triangle

(FIG 2). Dab the same coloured rouge in a line under the eyebrows, and smooth it in with a light layer of foundation. The colour should lie along the underside of the eyebrow, and fade down towards the eyesocket (FIG 1). With Pancake the foundation is now complete, but with Panstik it is now necessary to powder lightly. The most suitable powder is Max Factor C3–238, which does not alter the colour of the foundation in any way.

If highlighting is being used with Pancake, it must be applied before the foundation (see chapter 6). The highlight above the eyebrow used in most straight make-up is generally omitted with a Pancake foundation; partly because it is difficult to judge the correct position before the eyebrow has actually been painted, but mainly because in the smaller theatres for which Pancake is most suitable it is not really necessary.

FIG 2

Making up the eyes ✓

This begins with shading the eyelids to prevent them picking up too much light from overhead lighting. An unshaded eyelid usually looks very un-natural on the stage, and can give an extraordinarily predatory look to a character. The most natural colour for shading is a soft violet, rather the colour of a bruise, which is best achieved by blending Leichner dark blue liner and No. 3 carmine. Rub a little of each on the palm of your left hand, side by side, and blend them with the third finger of your right hand till a soft mauve-purple is achieved. With the same finger, spread it on the eyelids, and slightly out and up from the end of the eye (FIG 3). Wipe the finger clean and use it to soften the edges of the colour. Men may use as an alternative brown, grey or lake, but these must be used with discretion. They are best applied by rubbing them on the third finger of your hand, and not by apply-ing them straight to the eyelid. Women can, with various exceptions, wear any colour they choose, but it should be borne in mind that pale blue tends to look hard, and green malicious or spiteful (not always when worn by red-heads). This, of course, can be a help in characterisation. A colour that matches the costume that is being worn shows less than a contrasting one, as it looks like light reflected from the costume.

FIG 3

The next stage is the drawing in of the eye, which can be done with a brush loaded with black or brown greasepaint or Max Factor lining colour, or black Pancake, or with a black or brown eyebrow pencil (see chart p 12). The brush should be a proper make-up brush or (my preference) a No. 3 sable watercolour brush. An eyebrow pencil must be cleanly sharpened – some people prefer a chisel edge, some a normal point. Both have advantages.

If using a brush, load it by drawing it across the top of the stick of grease-paint or tin of lining colour. With black Pancake, wet the brush and draw it across the surface of the Pancake. Draw a line on your hand to see how heavy a line the brush will give, and load it more heavily with colour if necessary. Take the brush or pencil, and holding it at a right angle to your nose (the tip of the brush or pencil pointing to the nose) draw a fine line under the eye, starting below the inner corner of the white of the eye, about one-eighth of an inch below the roots of the eyelashes. Draw the line parallel to the eye-lashes until it reaches the lowest point of the eye, and then sweep slightly away and out, ending a quarter of an inch out from the outer end of the eye, and slightly below it (FIG 4). Do not follow the line of the lashes all the way and then take the line out (FIG 5). This closes up the eye when seen from a distance. The thickness of the line and the distance from the eye varies in

FIG 4

16

FIG 5

different sized theatres, and in differing styles of production (see chapter 4). Women, of course, can wear a heavier line than men.

Draw a line under the other eye in exactly the same way. Right-handed people usually start with the right eye, as with it the brush is held more easily in the correct position; holding the brush or pencil pointing towards the nose with the right hand under the left eye is more complicated, but it is quite possible.

Load your brush again with make-up, or take your pencil, and draw a heavier line along the top of the eye, starting at the beginning of the eyelashes at the inside of the eye and continuing as close as possible to the eyelashes right along the top of the eye, and then curving up and out for about one-third of an inch at the end of the eye. This curve out and up should be thickened with small brush strokes so that it forms a small curved triangle, based on the outer end of the eye (FIG 4). This represents the outward sweep of the upper eyelashes, and in a straight make-up it is essential that the lower corner of the triangle connects with the outer corner of the eye. Women may now apply artificial eyelashes if they are to be worn (see chapter 4).

Now apply mascara, which may be cake mascara applied with water, or one of the more recent cream mascaras which come complete with applicator. Brush the mascara on from the base of the eyelashes upwards, lifting the lashes quite clear of the eyes, and if artificial eyelashes are being worn, brushing the natural eyelashes into the artificial. Some women prefer to apply the mascara first, and then add the artificial lashes; in this way they do not become caked with mascara. When there is a line painted under the eye, it is not necessary to put mascara on the lower lashes.

Finally, with a clean orange-stick place a tiny dot of Leichner carmine 2 immediately below the naturally pink inside corner of each eye (FIG 4). This represents the pink corner that nature has provided, and also ties the lower painted line in with the real eye. In larger theatres, or if the eyes are wanted to be particularly bright, place a small dot or triangle of white greasepaint under the outer corner of the natural eye (FIG 4), using an orange-stick. This represents the light catching the outer corner of the white of the eye.

Making up the eyebrows ✓

For these I prefer to use black or brown greasepaint (see chart p 12) applied with an orange-stick. They can also be drawn with a black or brown eyebrow pencil, which is better for small theatres and cabaret but lacks the intensity needed for large theatres and opera houses.

The orange-stick can be loaded with colour by being drawn across the top of a stick of greasepaint or by being dug into the base of the stick, making a small hole in the centre. Use the flattened end of the orange-stick, which provides both a flat and a sharp edge with which to draw. As with the eyes, an eyebrow pencil can be sharpened to a chisel or rounded point. Hold the stick or eyebrow pencil along the top of the eyebrow with the point towards the bridge of the nose (FIG 6) and draw a line along the top of the eyebrow (on the eyebrow, not above it) and slightly past the highest point, continuing out and down slightly outside the natural eyebrow (FIG 7). This should give you a sharp outline, slightly exaggerating the shape of your own eyebrow. With light strokes of the orange-stick or pencil fill in under this line to the thickness that you require, being careful not to make the eyebrow too heavy, and bearing in mind that most eyebrows grow less thick as they

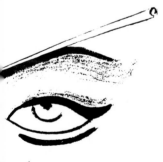

FIG 6

progress outward. Do not start the painting of the eyebrow any closer to
the bridge of the nose than the natural eyebrow. If the natural eyebrows are
very close together, leave the first quarter of an inch or so of the inside
ends unpainted. Draw in the second eyebrow in the same manner; you will
have the same problem holding the stick or pencil as when making up the eye.

For a normal straight make-up, the eyebrows should be drawn quite
lightly, without a great deal of greasepaint on the orange-stick. It is only by
practice that one can learn to judge the correct amount. If the eyebrows
appear too dark, powder lightly over them, using a small piece of cotton
wool not a powder puff, as the black is likely to come off on to it.

Making up the mouth ✓

To achieve a natural looking mouth (that is, one without lipstick) use
Leichner No. 8 (men) or No. 9 (women) greasepaint. Put a dab of greasepaint in the middle of the lower lip, and two dabs on the upper, either side
of the central cleft. Spread this over the mouth with a finger, working from
side to side of the lower lip, and from the centre out on the upper. Then put
two light dabs of carmine 3 on the upper lip and one of carmine 2 on
the lower, and spread these in the same way. Take care not to spread off the
natural area of the lips, unless you are deliberately changing the shape of the
mouth (see chapter 8), and keep the edge of the colour firm. A clearer outline
can be achieved by drawing a line around the mouth with a lipstick pencil,
and in large theatres (and in opera and ballet) it is usual to paint a very fine
black line around the mouth with an eye lining brush or an eyebrow pencil.
This gives definition to the lips without distorting the shape of the mouth.
If it is necessary to kiss someone during the performance, it is advisable to
powder the mouth lightly, again using a piece of cotton wool and not the
powder puff. There is a tradition of highlighting the upper lip with a white
outline, but in a straight make-up this usually looks as if the character has
been drinking milk and has not wiped his mouth.

Women frequently use their own lipstick, or one chosen to go with the
stage costume, and it must be very rare nowadays to meet a woman who is
not adept with a lipstick.

Highlighting ✓

Highlighting is the last thing applied in a make-up; it is always left until after
powdering, as the powder is apt to darken the pale colours that are used, and
also because the unpowdered grease catches the light and emphasises the
effect. This does not apply to a Pancake foundation (see final paragraph of
the section on foundation with Pancake).

With a straight make-up the only highlighting necessary is a touch of
Leichner No. 5 greasepaint above the eyebrow, which represents the light
catching the slight protuberance which most faces have above the natural
eyebrow. Take a clean orange-stick and load it with No. 5 greasepaint (in
the same way as loading a stick with black or brown for the eyebrow).
Draw a fairly light line just above the painted eyebrow and parallel with it,
starting approximately a quarter of an inch short of the inside point of the
painted eyebrow, and finishing a quarter of an inch before reaching the outside point (FIG 7). Smooth this in with the other end of the orange-stick,
or with the handle of the eyebrush. The highlight should be only about one-

FIG 7

eighth of an inch thick, and it should be well smoothed in, so that it does not lie like a stripe on the skin.

By following these rules, constant practice should produce a good straight make-up, one that could be used in a play by George Bernard Shaw, for example, in a moderately sized theatre, such as the Haymarket in London or the Playhouse in New York. By slightly exaggerating the details, such as heavier lines for the eyes and eyebrows, and by using brighter colours where recommended in the chart (p 12), the make-up would be suitable for a musical or an opera. Ballet make-up is usually even heavier. For a contemporary play in a small theatre, the eye and eyebrow details can be made lighter, and in a very small theatre omit the line under the eye, and merely darken the natural shape of the eyebrow.

In larger theatres there are two small additions that give extra radiance to the face: a small dab of carmine 3 on the lobes of the ears (traditional, and very effective), and a very light touch of the same colour above the outside corner of the eye, on the edge of the bone (FIG 7). The best way to apply these is with the finger that has spread the colour on the lips, before wiping it.

Removing make-up

Most make-up is removed by cream or oil. Max Factor and Leichner both make suitable liquidising creams, or any commercial cleansing cream can be used. Many performers use medicinal liquid paraffin, mainly because it is cheap, or olive oil, which is less greasy.

Before applying cream or grease, wipe away as much black as possible from around the eyes and the eyebrows, and red from the mouth, using a tissue or a piece of cotton wool. Then rub cream or oil liberally all over the face and neck, until the make-up is quite fluid. Wipe the hands clean, and with a tissue, or some cotton wool wrung out in warm water (I find this the most effective) wipe the face clean. Finally wash the face with soap and water. Many performers use a skin freshener or a cleansing lotion, either before or after washing.

4 · Eyes

Eyes are one of a performer's greatest assets, but to be fully exploited they have to be carefully defined and capable of conveying expression to the back of the theatre. This is not possible if they appear merely as two black smudges, or two small dots. It is essential that the shape of the eye is clearly drawn, and in such a way that the outline of the shape can be seen at a distance, without seeming too heavily painted from the closer seats.

The basic technique of painting the eye is discussed in chapter 3. This is easily adapted to larger or smaller theatres by being painted more or less heavily. To change the shape or character of the eye takes more adjustment.

Sunken eyes

To make the eyes seem sunken from age, exhaustion, or just to change the facial structure, shade more heavily around the eye socket. For age or exhaustion a No. 28 brown liner is the best colour to use but grey or, for a woman, violet, made by mixing No. 3 carmine and dark blue (see chapter 3), is also effective. The shading is applied before powdering on a grease or cream foundation, and before the foundation with Pancake or Panstick (see chapter 6). Spread the shading colour along the hollow above the upper eyelid and shade it up to the eyebrows and down over the eyelids, using a finger to spread it evenly. With the colour left on the finger, spread a softer shadow along immediately under the eye, so that the eye is in the middle of a circle of shading, the darkest section of the shading being in the hollow above the eye (FIG 8). The eyelines are then painted in the usual way. If a burning, haunted look is wanted, paint the eyelines more heavily than usual, and paint quite a heavy white dot at the outside corner of the eye.

FIG 8

Counteracting recessed eyes

To flatten out deeply recessed eyes, and for Oriental make-up, one uses highlights in much the same way as shadow was used in the preceding section. Use a No. 5 greasepaint before powdering with a grease or a cream foundation, and a white highlighting before the foundation with a Pancake or Panstik. If the finished effect is not strong enough, use further No. 5 after powdering. Shade the eyelids very lightly with the usual colour before painting the normal eyelines. With very deeply recessed eyes, take the highlighting right up to the eyebrows and on either side of the bridge of the nose.

Enlarging eyes, and making them smaller ✓

Small eyes can be easily enlarged by extending the eyelines further out from the end of the eye, by drawing the lower eyeline further down from the end of the eye, and by using heavier lines. Take great care that the lines still draw the shape of an eye (FIG 9). Fill in the outer corner of the painted eye with a lightly drawn white dot. Unless the eyes are set very widely apart, do not extend the eyes inward (that is, toward the bridge of the nose) as this can give a close eyed, shifty expression.

FIG 9

To make eyes seem smaller, reverse the process and use shorter, lighter lines, with the lower line close up against the eye, or entirely eliminated. In a small theatre, using only mascara, with no eyelining at all, will shrink the eyes considerably.

Eyes closer together and further apart

For purposes of characterisation one may desire closely set eyes (to suggest untrustworthiness) or eyes set wide apart (to suggest innocence). For the first of these start the eyelines slightly inward from the natural eye and do not carry them beyond the outer edge of the real eye. Paint the red dot inwards from the natural eye, and not below it as in a straight make-up (FIG 10).

To widen the eyes, begin the lines below the inside edge of the pupil and carry them well out, with a wider sweep than usual. Place the red dot below the inside white of the eye, and use a fairly generous white dot in the outer corner of the painted eye (FIG 11). Be careful not to exaggerate this effect, as it is easy to give an impression of being cross-eyed.

Rounder and narrower eyes

A round-eyed, surprised expression is easily achieved by using short, thick

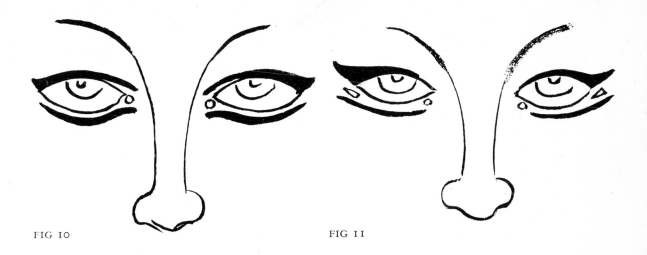

FIG 10   FIG 11

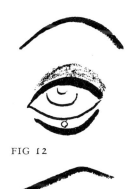

FIG 12

FIG 13

lines above and below the eye, taking care not to carry them past the outer edges of the natural eye. A marked curve to the lower line adds to the surprised or pop-eyed expression. Do not use any white at the end of the eye, but put a small dot inside the lower line below the pupil. Take care not to extend the eyelid shadow past the end of the natural eye (FIG 12).

A long narrow eye is achieved by thin lines carried well out past the natural eye, with the lower eyeline painted close against the lower eyelashes. The eyelid shadow should be carried well out past the natural eye, and if a white dot is used it should be placed at the end of the natural eye, and not below it, as in a straight make-up. Take care not to curve the upper eyeline too strongly upwards at the outer end (FIG 13).

Artificial eyelashes

These are frequently worn in the theatre, and come in a variety of types from those so light as to be almost invisible to the extremely heavy lashes usually worn by dancers. For a straight make-up, the short thick lashes made from fur are the most useful. These emphasise the shape of the natural eye and make the movements of the eyelid carry more clearly in the theatre. It is unnecessary, I hope, to say that artificial eyelashes are normally worn only by women on the stage.

Most artificial eyelashes carry instructions for application on the box in which they are sold. Some are self-adhesive, others have an adhesive supplied with them. If additional adhesive is required, various rubber solutions can be bought for the purpose. The lashes must be trimmed to the correct length; both the length of the actual hairs and the overall length of the base. This should reach from where the natural upper eyelashes begin to the end of the eye. If the artificial lashes are taken closer to the nose than the natural lashes, they will make the eyes appear close-set, and if they extend past the natural end of the eye they will work loose with the movement of the eyelid. Occasionally in a stylised or fantastic make-up the lashes can be very effective sweeping upward and out from the natural eye, and in this case they should leave the line of the natural eyelashes about a quarter of an inch before the end, and curve upwards from there.

The length of the hairs in the artificial lashes depends on the effect required. For a sultry temptress, or for a stylised make-up and in ballet, long lashes are necessary. For a straight make-up, and in a small theatre, quite short ones are sufficient. The lashes are usually cut in a curve, with the eyelashes on the outside end rather longer than the inside. Remember that the outside end is on the right for one lash and on the left for the other, and do not cut the two lashes as if they were to be worn on the same eye.

The lashes should be applied from the inside of the eye outwards. If adhesive is used, apply it to the base of the lashes, *never* to the eyelids. Apply the inside end of the base (the end with the shorter lashes) close to the roots of the natural lashes and press the base along the roots of the lashes to the end of the eye. Make sure that the base is placed in such a way that the lashes curve out and up and do not come down over the eye. This sometimes takes practice. An orange-stick is a great help in pressing the base of the lashes into place and ensuring that it sticks firmly.

Artificial lashes can be used to stress special effects in eye make-up. They help make an eye look larger, but they should not be worn when attempting to make an eye look smaller. By cutting the base shorter than the natural eye they can help a round-eyed effect, and by using lashes with long hairs and cutting the hairs at the inside end quite short, so that the lashes are wedge-shaped, they will help to lengthen an eye.

It can be seen that eyes can be altered in many ways quite simply. Constant practice is necessary to achieve clear, unsmudged drawing of the lines. Eventually one can achieve many effects, such as tipping the eyes upwards by drawing the lines from below the inside corner of the eyes to above the outside (FIG 14); tipping them downwards by bringing the outside ends of the two eyelines down instead of up (FIG 15) and other effects as required. To strengthen these effects in a large theatre, or in opera and ballet, an extra line can be drawn representing the fold at the top of the eyelid, extending it in the direction of the eye make-up (FIGS 14 and 15).

FIG 14

FIG 15

5 · Eyebrows ✓

The eyebrows play a major part in facial expression. One has only to think of the masks of comedy and tragedy, or the traditional face of Pierrot, to realise how important they can be. An incorrectly painted eyebrow can change the whole character of a face in repose, and so give a different, and possibly incorrect, slant to a characterisation.

As a rough generalisation, eyebrows that slope downwards from the centre suggest sadness or peevishness, strongly curved eyebrows vivacity or archness, and eyebrows rising upwards from the centre devilishness or ruthlessness. The eyebrow that usually creates the most natural effect (and is therefore the most expressive without distortion) is one that slopes upward for two-thirds of its length and then turns sharply downward for the remaining third (FIG 7). The highest point of the eyebrow should be well outside the area immediately above the pupil of the eye – if possible, it should be above the outside end of the natural eye. This cannot be stressed too strongly. Eyebrows painted with the highest point close in by the nose give a most unfortunate expression to the face.

It is important that the eyebrow is painted along the line of the natural eyebrow and not separately, above it, unless an exaggerated or unnatural effect is required (the technique of painting eyebrows is discussed in chapter 3). Natural eyebrows lie along a fold of muscle, and when one paints away from this it creates many problems.

Raising low eyebrows

Performers occasionally have thick heavy eyebrows, which from a distance seem to rest on the eye beneath them. This is generally a male problem, as women normally pluck their eyebrows to an ideal shape and remove the problem at its source. Many male performers with low or heavy eyebrows have them lightly plucked, but if this is not desired, there are several solutions. The easiest, which is very effective in large theatres, is to brush the lower half of the eyebrow lightly with Leichner No. 5 or Lit K and then draw the painted eyebrow along the upper half of the natural eyebrow.

In smaller theatres, it is necessary to blot out the natural eyebrow more effectively, and this is traditionally done with a damp cake of toilet soap, which is pressed over the eyebrow until it sticks flat to the face. The drawback to this method is that it eventually bleaches the eyebrows to an unbecoming shade of ginger, if it is used every night for a long period. The preparations used for stiffening Edwardian moustaches will stick down eyebrows quite effectively without bleaching them, and in England a preparation called Pomade Hongroise, which is supplied in small tubes, is used a great deal. Whatever is used, it should be applied before the foundation, which is then painted right over it. This leaves a fairly smooth surface on which can be applied normal shading, and the eyebrows can be drawn wherever required. One must still take care, particularly in a straight make-up, to relate them to the natural eyebrow.

This technique of sticking down the natural eyebrow can be applied to the outer end of the eyebrow when the painted line is so exaggerated as to leave the natural brow completely, but it is not necessary in large theatres where the natural hairs will be sufficiently hidden by the shading of Leichner No. 8 or 9 (described in chapter 3). Nor is it necessary when the painted line closely parallels the natural eyebrow.

Emphasising the eyebrows

Eyebrows can be emphasised by drawing them in with a heavier colour – using more actual greasepaint on the orange-stick, or heavier strokes of the pencil – or by drawing them in a thicker shape. This must be approached with care, as it can easily turn into a George Robey effect. Eyebrows can be emphasised structurally by using a heavier or darker coloured shadow beneath them, and a stronger highlight above them, which makes them appear to jut out, and gives a craggy look to the face. Most wigmakers will supply made-up eyebrows to be stuck on with spirit gum if an extremely bushy effect is desired. This can also be achieved by using a small amount of crêpe, carefully teased out and stuck on (see chapter 16).

White and pale blonde eyebrows

White, grey and blonde eyebrows are always difficult to make-up successfully, as lighting and distance tend to make them disappear entirely. Unless
a performer is an extremely pale blonde, it is better to use a medium brown
for the eyebrows. For a woman it is essential, unless she is playing a character who would not wear make-up at all (such as an eighteenth-century
Swedish peasant girl). Fortunately men are not usually as fair as women. For
the rare, extremely fair man (or a performer in a very pale blonde wig) draw
the eyebrows in very lightly with a light brown eyebrow pencil, and then
draw a heavier line beneath them to represent the shadow that they cast.
This is best drawn with a slightly darker pencil (FIG 16).

FIG 16

This same technique is used for white eyebrows, which are frequently
rather bushy when they occur in nature. Paint the eyebrow with heavy
strokes of an orange-stick charged with white greasepaint (Leichner No. 22)
and then draw a grey or black line under it, using either an eyebrow pencil,
or greasepaint on an orange-stick. If a bushy effect is required, draw shading
lines upward into the white painted area – these lines, of course, will be the
same colour as the line already drawn beneath the eyebrow.

Grey eyebrows can be drawn with a grey pencil or grey greasepaint, and
emphasised by shading beneath them with black. They are rather an unnecessary refinement, as in most theatres the difference between grey and
black does not carry to any extent. A good effect of bushy iron-grey eyebrows
can be achieved by painting strokes of white on to a black eyebrow, using
an orange-stick charged with white greasepaint (FIG 17), or by rubbing the
natural eyebrows the wrong way with white or grey greasepaint.

FIG 17

The muscular movement of eyebrows

One must always take the muscular action of the eyebrows into account, and
it is a good idea when trying a new make-up to practise expressions in front
of a mirror, and see exactly what happens to the eyebrows under performance
conditions. Many a performer has painted Mephistophelian eyebrows on to
his face without allowing for muscle movement, and then lifted the centre of
his eyebrows to achieve a dramatic effect, resulting in a rather querulous
'V' over each eye.

There is a tradition (especially in opera) of painting the centre of the
eyebrows some way above the natural eyebrow. This gives the most extraordinary effect from a distance – something between boredom and acute
distaste. Carried to an extreme, it can give an effect of deep sorrow. Singers
in particular have to be on their guard against this mistake, as at least seventy-
five per cent of them lift the centre of their eyebrows as soon as they begin
to sing (the remaining twenty-five per cent either depress them or leave them
unmoved). To counteract this tendency it is necessary to paint the eyebrow
at a steeper angle than normal, cutting obliquely across the natural eyebrow
(FIG 18). This will give a completely natural effect on the stage, but it can
look rather odd at close quarters.

It can be seen that every face poses its own problems with eyebrows.
Constant practice and trying expressions in front of a mirror (or the advice
of a trusted friend in the audience) will overcome difficulties, and an eyebrow
closely related to the natural eyebrow will never be disastrously unsuitable.

FIG 18

6 · Shading and highlighting ✓

The contours of the face can be emphasised, altered or counteracted by the proper use of highlights and shading. The normal effect of a shadow is to recess the area over which it is applied, and of a highlight to make the area more prominent. Thus a shapeless small nose, for example, can be given classical proportions by shading along both sides and judicious highlighting along the centre (described in chapter 7). In the days of overall flat lighting it was customary to shade and highlight faces in a simple straight make-up, to counteract the flattening effect of the lights. This custom is still often used even with the most advanced directional lighting, producing some very odd effects of over-emphasis of the facial structure. A well-shaped face on a well-lit stage needs shading only immediately below the eyebrows and on the eyelids, and these are coloured shadings (see chapter 3), not just shadows as such.

Many performers have a structural detail that they want to improve – shortening a nose or strengthening a chin – and this is legitimately achieved by subtle use of shading. Shading is also used to age the face, to show the effect of tiredness or exhaustion, and to change the basic structure of the face – slimming a fat face and so on. Shading and highlighting are always used in conjunction with each other. In nature there is never a shadow without a complementary highlight, and in make-up we must simulate the same effect.

Techniques of shading and highlighting ✓
As described in the sections on foundations in chapter 3, shading is applied to cream and grease foundations *before* powdering, and highlights *after* powdering. With a Pancake foundation, shadings and highlights are the first thing to be applied, and the foundation is painted over them. With Panstik they can be applied either in the method used with cream and grease, or in the same way as with Pancake.

Large areas of shading and highlights with cream and grease foundations ✓
The most effective colour for large areas of shading (under chins, along the sides of noses and for hollows in cheeks, etc.) is a mixture of Leichner No. 8 and No. 3 green. This gives a muddy, rather turgid, colour which blends very well with all flesh foundations and seems to absorb light, so that solid areas of flesh painted with it seem, from a reasonable distance, to disappear. Like all shading, it must be used with discretion, and always be carefully blended into the foundation. Mix the two colours on the palm of the left hand, and use a finger to apply them to the necessary areas, carefully fading the edge of the colour into the foundation (suggested uses of shading are discussed later in this chapter). Deeper hollows in a shaded area are achieved by thicker application of the shading colour over the area required. When the shading is completed, powder, and continue the make-up as described in chapter 3.

Highlights are usually applied as the last thing in a make-up, but can, if desired, be applied before making up the eyes and eyebrows. As a general rule the best colour to use is Leichner No. 5, a yellowish, pale flesh colour. For a very intense highlight over a small area, use Leichner No. 1 or No. 2.

Apply the grease to a fingertip and lightly spread it over the area required. By their nature, highlights are usually smaller than shadows – a large area of shading on a plump cheek will be emphasised by a much smaller highlight on the cheek-bone. Highlights have much sharper edges than shadows, so it is not as necessary to blend the colour into the foundation – just as well, as it is not easy to blend greasepaint into a powdered surface. A more subtle highlight can be achieved for small theatres by applying the No. 5 before powdering, and using a colourless powder (Max Factor Translucent). If the effect is not strong enough, add an extra touch of No. 5 to the centre of the highlight after powdering.

Shading and highlighting with a Pancake foundation
The simplest form of shading with a Pancake foundation is to paint the area required with a darker coloured Pancake – Negro 2 for men, and A.L. for women – and then apply the usual coloured Pancake foundation over it. A certain amount of highlighting can be obtained by rubbing a damp piece of cottonwool (or a wet finger) over the required area, and wiping away some of the Pancake, allowing the natural colour to show through. This, of course, would not work with a very pale foundation. This technique of shading and highlighting is very suitable for shading under chins (essential for most singers) and for slimming an over-round face, but it is not very subtle, and not really suited to character make-up. For this, shading and highlights are painted directly on to the face, before the foundation, using Max Factor lining colours – Shading (743), (or Shading (1363) under a pale make-up), and White (12) for highlighting. These are applied with a brush, and do not require any great subtlety or shading in – they should almost resemble a graph for a make-up. The face is then powdered with talc to set the lining colours, and the normal Pancake foundation is applied over it. The covering of Pancake softens and blends the shading and highlighting beneath it, so that what starts out as a crude diagram finishes as a subtle shading. One can also shade Pancake with Shader Dry rouge, applied either with a rouge mop or with the technique described in chapter three for applying dry rouge to the cheeks.

Uses of shading and highlighting
The basic uses are for improving on nature, changing the structure of the face to suit a racial type or a special character, or changing the age group of the face. Most of these are discussed in the various chapters on separate features and character make-up, but we can see here how to alter the basic overall shape of the face – lengthening and slimming a round face, and shortening and widening a long face. The first is often needed in opera, as both soprano and tenor voices frequently come from round, plump faces and short necks. As these are the voices most favoured by composers for romantic roles, art must come to the aid of nature.

Slimming and lengthening the face
The first stage is to shade fairly lightly down both sides of the face, fading out on the line of the jawbone. Paint a heavier shading under the cheekbones, making sure that it does not have a hard edge (FIG 19). Under the chin and the neck should be shaded as described in chapter 9. Unless the nose is already prominent, it should be evenly shaded down both sides and high-

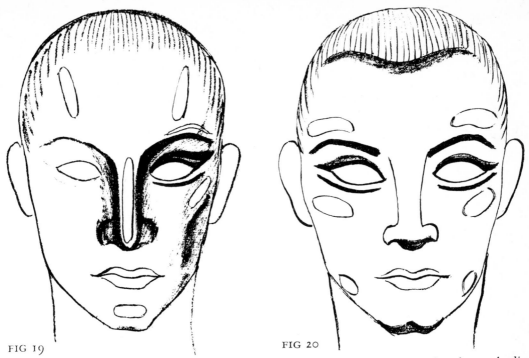

FIG 19

FIG 20

lighted in the centre, as described in chapter 7. The eye and eyebrow shading should be normal, but on a very flat face an extra shadow in a deeper colour (violet, brown or lake) can be painted along the hollow at the top of the eyelid.

Highlights should be applied on the point of the chin, on the cheekbones, above the eyebrows and, as mentioned before, on the nose (FIG 19). All this helps to lengthen the face, and take away from the roundness, and if the eyebrows are painted at a slightly sharper angle than usual this will help even further. An example of the use of this type of shading in opera can be seen in the photos of Alberto Remedios in *Der Freischutz* (pls 19, 21).

A simpler form of slimming the face can be achieved by just shading under the cheekbones and along the side of the nose, and highlighting the cheekbones, nose and chin. This is often used by performers whose faces, although structurally sound, are a little too plump.

Shortening and widening the face

This is required less often than lengthening a face, and it is more difficult to achieve. One of the greatest aids is a wig designed to come considerably lower than the natural hairline. Failing this, the hairline can be painted lower either with eyebrow pencil or with greasepaint or a lining colour on an orange-stick. Choose a colour as close to the natural colour of the hair as possible, and paint it in with fine strokes of the pencil or orange-stick. Shade the point of the chin with an inverted 'V' shape, to blunt it, and paint a large, smooth, horizontal highlight above the eyebrow, in place of the small highlight used in a straight make-up. Shade under the tip of the nose, and use horizontal highlights well out on the cheekbones and on the widest point of the jawbone (FIG 20). The eyebrows can be painted more horizontally than usual to add to the effect, and the cheek colour should be painted well out on the face, leaving an area of the foundation colour between it and the nose.

27

Regularising the face

All these suggestions have been affecting the whole face. Most faces are not by nature even, and distance and lighting can accentuate the irregularities. These can be easily corrected by judicious use of shading and highlights – a nose that leans to one side can be shaded on that side, and a highlight painted where the true line of the nose should lie. Too long a nose can be shortened and a crooked jawline can be straightened by the same means.

Lines and wrinkles

These are very rarely well painted. One usually sees a thin line of lake with an equally thin line of No. 5 painted beside it as a highlight. This quite ignores the fact that wrinkles usually lie at the bottom of a fold or indentation in the face, and not just flat on the surface. The sort of wrinkle that is just a crack in the surface would not be seen from any distance; the wrinkles that carry are those deeply indented into the face. The structure of an ageing face is discussed in chapter 12, but here we can describe the technique of painting wrinkles and lines.

FIG 21

First, wherever possible, paint wrinkles WHERE THEY FALL ON YOUR OWN FACE. This makes the natural muscle action of the face add to the effect of the make-up, and not counteract it. Start the painting of the wrinkle with a shading of lake along the total area of the required indentation, about a quarter of an inch wide, and shade it in with a fingertip. For a more weather-beaten effect, paint the wrinkles in with the mixture of Leichner No. 8 and No. 3 Green described in Chapter 6, with a centre line of brown, drawn with an eyebrow pencil. Then draw a narrower line of blue or brown along the centre of the indentation and fade it in rather less, so that you have a shaded area with a narrower dark centre. Powder, and apply a highlight of No. 5 parallel to, but not quite touching, the wrinkle or line, and smaller in area (FIG 21). This should be applied with an orangestick, and smoothed lightly in. When using Pancake foundation both the shadow and the highlight should be painted first – the shading with Max Factor Shading (734 or 1363) lining colour and the highlighting with White (12) – and then powdered with talc before applying the Pancake.

When the entire make-up is complete, check the effects of the wrinkles, and deepen them where necessary with a brown or black pencil or with a very little black or brown greasepaint on a fine brush. This must be done very carefully and lightly, or the result will be grotesque. This final deepening here and there gives the effect of uneven depth that occurs in wrinkles where the muscle pull is strongest. If you must depart from the natural structure of the face, then the painting must be done with even greater care, and the shading blended well in so that there is no sudden edge or break.

Wrinkles can be used most effectively to disguise a wig join. This is discussed in chapter 16, and it is well illustrated by the photograph of Sir Donald Wolfit as Lear (pl 25).

7 · Noses

The making-up of noses is haunted by a variety of mistaken ideas left over from the days of flat lighting on stages. Judging by some of the make-up one sees, one is tempted to say from the days of gas lighting. It should be borne in mind that a well-shaped nose on a properly lit stage needs no shading or highlighting for a straight make-up. There is no reason, under any conditions, to paint parallel lines down the nose like a tram track. These – which are worn surprisingly frequently – detract from the shape of the nose, and mystify the closer members of the audience, who must occasionally wonder if they are part of a ritualistic disguise.

Altering the shape of the nose
Altering the shape of the nose follows the basic rules of make-up – shading removes and highlighting adds. To make a snub nose longer and more classical in shape, shade along either side of the nose using one of the shading techniques described in chapter 6, and highlight the centre of the nose (FIG 22). If the nose turns up at the end, do not carry the highlight all the way down to the tip, and if you want to lengthen the nose, highlight under the actual tip of the nose. Additional lengthening can also be achieved by carrying the highlighting up to between the eyebrows. This can also be used on a normal nose to achieve the effect of a Grecian profile – paint the highlighting from slightly above the eyebrows to halfway down the nose.

To shorten a nose, shade across the tip of the nose, and emphasise this with a small highlight across the nose immediately above the shadow. To recess a high bridge on a nose, lightly shade across the actual area of the bridge, and to achieve the effect of a Roman nose, highlight very strongly immediately below the bridge and shade either side of the highlighting (FIG 23).

To widen the nostrils, highlight the widest portion of them and then paint the inside edge of the nostrils with lake. To make a large nose less prominent, paint the entire nose very slightly darker than the rest of the face

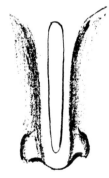

FIG 22

FIG 23

29

king care to blend the darker colour well into the foundation where the nose joins the cheek) and then apply shading as necessary to shorten or narrow it. Do not highlight, except perhaps for a small highlight to mark the altered length of the nose.

Crooked or broken noses can easily be straightened by shading on the protruding side and using a highlight in a straight line where the centre of the nose should lie. In reverse, a straight nose can be made to appear crooked by distorted shading and a crooked highlight. Noses with no definite shape can be given one by firm shading along the sides and, if necessary, central highlighting.

All these effects are achieved purely by painting, and many of them really only achieve their objective when the face is viewed straight on. To change the actual profile, and for extreme effects, it is necessary to use nose putty. The technique for using this is described in chapter 16. Except in very large theatres, nose putty must be used with great discretion – a little goes a very long way. With nose putty there is no limit to the effects that can be achieved where noses are concerned. Look at the photographs of Sir Laurence Olivier – a superb exponent of make-up – as Macbeth and Caesar (pls 10, 11) and Orson Welles as Othello (pl 4), and at the fantastic nose worn by Edith Coates as the old Countess in *The Queen of Spades* (pl 17). This is an extreme make-up intended for the vast spaces of the Royal Opera House, Covent Garden.

With putty the nose can be lengthened, heightened or widened, but always check on the effect from the side with two mirrors, and make sure that the weight of the putty is not going to disturb your performance. Make sure also that the foundation is evenly applied over the putty, and that the edges of the putty are well smoothed in, and do not have a visible ridge where they join the face.

8 · Mouths

Enlarging the mouth

The shape of the mouth is shown more by the colour than by the structure, which allows greater freedom in changing the shape for the stage. The simplest way of making a mouth larger is to paint it to the size required, and, in large theatres, to outline it more strongly in lake or in black than if the natural contour was being used. If a very heavy mouth is required, when nature has only provided a normal or thin mouth, it is necessary to shade under the outline of the painted lower lip, and to highlight the edge of both lips to simulate the structure of a heavy mouth (FIG 24). Quite a strong shadow is needed, either brown or black, lightly sketched in with a brush or pencil. The highlight on a cream or grease foundation should be No. 5 greasepaint, and it should be well smoothed in, so that it does not appear as a stripe of yellow.

FIG 24

A rather loose, sexy, look can be given to a mouth by highlighting the centre of the lower lip with No. 5 greasepaint and not altering the make-up in any other way (FIG 25).

FIG 25

Making the mouth smaller ✓

To diminish a mouth, cover the entire lip area with foundation, and then paint in the mouth to the size required. A small mouth needs to be clearly defined, or it will not carry. In a large theatre outline it with black. It may be necessary to shadow slightly the unused portion of the natural mouth, using a very little of the mixture of Leichner No. 8 and green greasepaint. A mouth can be painted right over with foundation, and no colour used at all, which gives a very mean, hard, effect to a straight make-up, and is also very effective on a face made up to look old.

Weak mouths

Weakness is not so easy to convey in make-up, as anything that is too in-indefinite does not carry to the audience. A weak mouth is usually loose and not clearly defined, and is best achieved by painting a fairly large mouth without outlining it, and possibly painting a highlight of Leichner No. 5 on the lower lip. Many weak mouths, and those of mentally retarded people, are surprisingly red, and have a constant wet look which can be simulated by oiling or greasing the lips after they are made up. This makes the colour wipe off very easily, and it is not recommended if the play requires any kissing. A discontented look can be added to a weak mouth by painting short black or brown lines diagonally downward for about a quarter of an inch from the ends of the mouth. Do not try and achieve a happy expression by painting short lines upwards from the corners of the mouth – this gives a look of imbecility.

Aged mouths and illness

Illness and age are best represented by pale mouths. There is a tradition of old mouths being painted in lake, but this is inclined to look artificial. In nature it is usually only the dark, blotchy, type of elderly face that has a dark mouth; most old mouths are pale and withered. They can be painted in various colours ranging in tone from Leichner No. 8 or 9 through to No. 5, but this is rather extreme used by itself. Dabs of No. 5 on a mouth painted with No. 8 or 9 can give a most effective puckered look (FIG 26). This can be taken further for a very old face, and puckers of brown or lake (in a very large theatre, strengthened with black) painted radiating inwards over the mouth, with highlights of No. 5 between them (FIG 27). As mentioned earlier, simply painting over the mouth with the foundation can give a very convincing aged look.

FIG 26

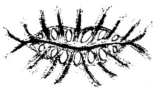

FIG 27

Toothlessness or gappy teeth can be simulated by painting out the teeth with tooth enamel, which is made by both Leichner and Max Factor. A convincing aged look can be given by painting an uneven line along the edge of the teeth, as if they were worn down, and by occasional jagged gaps, as if a tooth had broken diagonally across. Painting out all the teeth is not very convincing, as the mouth does not have the sunken look which goes with no teeth, but this can be partly achieved by painting the mouth out with foundation and then lightly shading the whole mouth area with either the mixture of No. 8 and green, or with brown, which recesses the painted area.

Illness is best shown by a slightly paler mouth than normal. For a woman, one of the pale pink lipsticks gives an effect of being made up and also being slightly unwell. If a pink lipstick is not available, use a mixture of carmine 3 and white. For a man, a faint smear of No. 5 spread over the made-up mouth with one finger gives a convincing effect. This gives the effect of a veil over the colour, and is more effective than using a paler colour.

Cabaret and revue

For women these present no problem, as a strongly coloured lipstick is taken for granted, but for a man it is more difficult. Using No. 8 or 9 greasepaint alone, not adding carmine as in a straight make-up, is the simplest answer. A better effect is achieved by using Max Factor Moist Rouge Brown Red (9), which gives the most natural lip colour of any make-up. A mouth with no make-up at all looks very unnatural with a painted face; the combination of artificial and natural colour is nearly always unfortunate, either in artificial or natural light.

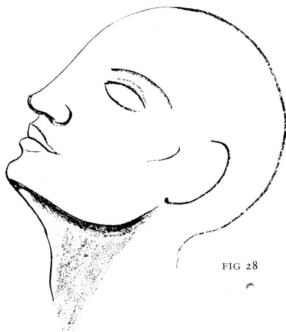

FIG 28

9 · Chins

Chins present a number of problems on the stage. Many performers have either not enough or too much chin, and both of these are aggravated by lighting and distance. Singers mostly have over-developed muscles under the chin, which can make their faces look as if they slide straight into the neck. Where, with noses, it is possible to add to the shape with putty, with chins it is not practicable (except for extreme effects, such as witches) as the putty is apt to be disturbed by the muscle action around the chin, although I have known of a prima ballerina who always wore a small plastic chin on the stage.

Emphasising the chin

This is done by using quite heavy shading under the jawline. With a cream or grease foundation use a mixture of Leichner No. 8 and No. 3 green, and with Pancake or Panstik use Negro 2 for men and A.L. for women. The shading should come right up to the jawbone (or where the jawbone is desired to appear) and should be faded out fairly sharply. It is taken to about halfway down the neck, where it is gradually faded out. The overall shading is roughly diamond-shaped (FIG 28). Be careful, especially with women, not

1   A demonstration make-up for Othello by Douglas Young of the Max Factor London Salon

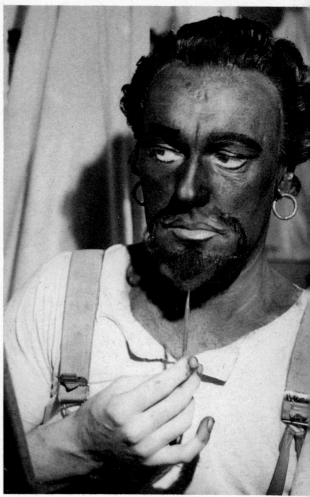

2 Jon Vickers as Otello in Verdi's *Otello*,
Covent Garden, 1961

3 Sir Ralph Richardson making up as
Othello in the Old Vic production, 1938

4 Orson Welles as Othello, St James's, 1951

5 Richard Burton as Othello, Old Vic, 1956

6 Sir Laurence Olivier as Othello, National
Theatre, 1964

7 Sir Laurence Olivier as himself, 1964

8 Sir Laurence Olivier as Coriolanus, Old Vic, 1938   9 Sir Laurence Olivier as Hamlet, Old Vic, 1937

10   Sir Laurence Olivier as Macbeth, Old Vic, 1937

11　Sir Laurence Olivier as Caesar in *Caesar and Cleopatra*, St James's, 1951

12 Sir Laurence Olivier in *The Master Builder*, National Theatre, 1965

13   Sir Laurence Olivier in *Venus Observed*, St James's, 1950

15 Rae Woodland as Odabella in Verdi's
Attila, Sadler's Wells, 1963

14 Maureen Guy as she looked to the
audience in Saint-Saens' *Samson and
Delilah*, Sadler's Wells, 1963

16 Close up of Maureen Guy as Delilah

17 Edith Coates as the Countess in Tchaikovsky's *The Queen of Spades*, Covent Garden, 1951

18 Don Garrard as Attila in Verdi's *Attila*, Sadler's Wells, 1964

19　Alberto Remedios as Max in Weber's
　　Der Freischutz, Sadler's Wells, 1963

20　Alberto Remedios as himself

21　Alberto Remedios as he looked to the
　　audience in *Der Freischutz*

22 A demonstration make-up for a Japanese girl by Douglas Young of the Max Factor London Salon

23 Chinese theatre: the Monkey Emperor
wears an elaborate traditional make-up

24 Chinese theatre: a court lady wearing
the traditional make-up for a young girl

25   Sir Donald Wolfit as Lear, 1965

26 Sir Michael Redgrave as Prospero in
The Tempest, Stratford-on-Avon, 1951

27 Paul Rogers as Lear, Old Vic, 1957

28   Paul Scofield as Sir Thomas More in *A Man for All Seasons*, Globe, 1960

30   Robert Helpmann as Richard III, Old Vic, 1957

31   Vivien Leigh as Cleopatra in *Caesar and Cleopatra*, St James's, 1951

33 Dame Edith Evans in *The Dark is Light Enough*, Aldwych, 1954

35 Dame Edith Evans as Margaret in
Richard III, Stratford-on-Avon, 1961

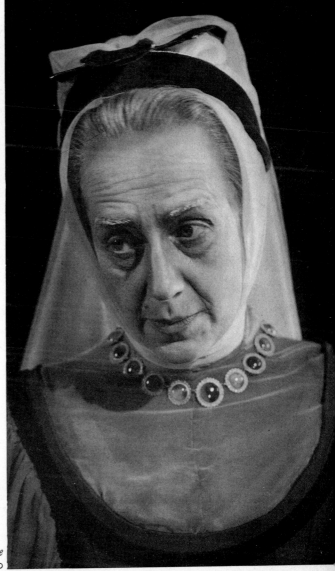

36 Dame Peggy Ashcroft as Paulina in *The
Winter's Tale*, Stratford-on-Avon, 1960

38 Patrick Allen as King Arthur in *Island of the Mighty*, Aldwych Theatre, 1973.

39 The foundation with colour shading and slight corrective shading to the nose

40 The line under the eye

41 The line above the eye

42 The eyebrows

43 The face without make-up

44 The finished make-up, with mouth, mascara on eyelashes and highlighting

45

45/46 Designs by Timothy O'Brien for the two
clowns in the Sadler's Wells 1962 production
of *The Bartered Bride*, showing the suggested
make-up

46

to make the shading too heavy, or it will look like a beard. Further emphasis can be given to the chin by a highlight following the line of the jawbone, immediately above the upper edge of the shading. This is only recommended where a very pronounced jaw is required, as the highlight has an extremely strong effect.

A slightly receding chin can be strengthened by a highlight on the point of the chin and, if necessary, a slight shadow just below it.

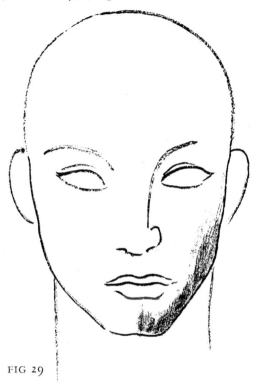

FIG 29

Subduing a strong jaw
This is harder than emphasising a weak jaw, and not usually as successful. It is done by a carefully graduated shading, beginning under the cheek-bones and spreading down over the entire jaw, fading out on the line of the jaw-bone. The shading can be even over the whole line of the jawbone, or stronger in some places, depending on the shape of the original jaw and the final effect that is required: a heavier shadow, within reason, recesses the area more strongly (FIG 29). It is essential that the shading blends well with the tone of the foundation (use the same colours that are suggested for strengthening the jaw) and is not too heavy, or it will look like beard stubble on the jaw. A highlight of Leichner No. 5 applied before powdering *under* the line of the jawbone can also help to soften the effect of an over-emphasised chin, and can be used without any shading to soften a chin that is too sharp, without being too heavy. The highlight should be brought right to the edge of the jawline, where it is faded out quite sharply. The lower edge is faded into the neck foundation at the base of the chin. A too pointed jaw can be softened by an inverted 'V' shape painted on the point of the chin, giving a hint of a cleft chin, and softening the overall line. For men, this is very effective painted in dark blue (a Leichner dark blue liner), which gives a faint effect of beard stubble in the cleft.

Creating double chins and sagging jowls

The jawline is one of the first places to show approaching age, usually with an indentation below each end of the mouth, running down to each side of the chin, with a slight sagging of the cheek or jowl outside of it. This can be achieved by two inverted 'V'-shaped shadows painted on the jawline either side of the chin, with the points coming almost up to the ends of the mouth, and a curving highlight starting outside the mouth and coming down over the line of the jawbone, and round and up towards the ear (FIG 30). The strongest section of the highlight is the downward sweep from the mouth to under the jawbone. It then softens, and fades out entirely well below the ear. This gives a convincing sag to the sides of the face, and can be added to by a simulated double chin, achieved by highlighting. If you press your chin down to your neck, you will get a fold of flesh, and it is the centre of this that should be highlighted. A shadow painted in the crease below the highlight will add to the effect, and a further highlight can be placed below, on the Adam's apple. Spreading the highlights as widely as possible horizontally will help to thicken the neck.

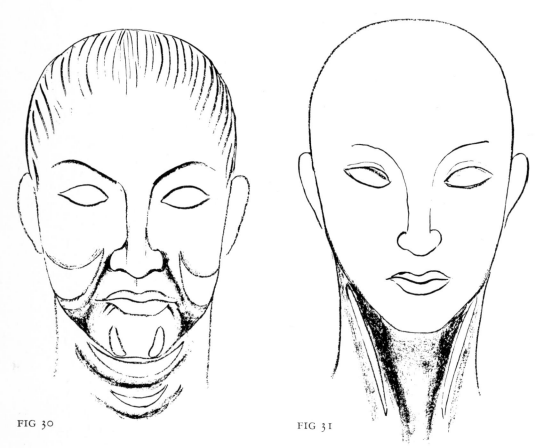

FIG 30   FIG 31

Slimming a thick neck

This can also be done with highlights and shadows. Paint a shading under the chin, as if emphasising the chin, and carry it downwards in two tails on either side of the Adam's apple. The thick cords of muscle on either side of this can have a long perpendicular highlight on each of them, and a perpendicular shading, starting under the ear, can be brought down on either side of these highlights (FIG 31). If the costume has a low enough neckline, the 'salt cellars' can be shaded in, which helps a great deal to lengthen the neck.

Removing double chins and sagging jowls

These are painted out with the same technique used in emphasising the chin. In both cases one should try to restore the original firm line of the jawbone, painting the shading up to this line and shading away unwanted sagging folds of flesh or muscle. If necessary, highlight the original line of the jawbone before powdering, which will stress it without over-exaggerating it.

Changing character

By manipulating these various techniques, a number of character changes can be made to the face. Emphasising the chin adds to a strong, pugnacious, characterisation, while subduing it will add to an indecisive one. A sharp pointed chin (achieved by a strong highlight on the point of the chin, with a shadow immediately below it) will help an inquisitive, interfering characterisation, and so on. Always make sure that the shadow under the chin blends imperceptibly into the neck, and does not look like a chin-strap.

Beard stubble on the chin

A light effect of stubble is achieved with a cream or grease foundation by blending a little dark blue liner in with the foundation. With Pancake, a very light uneven coat of Brownish/Black will give much the same effect. This should be applied with a damp sponge wrung out until it is almost dry. For a heavier effect of stubble, mix a little black with the blue for a cream or grease foundation, and with Pancake use a slightly heavier dabbing of Brownish/Black, or alternatively sketch it in with an eyebrow pencil. Make sure that the area of stubble blends imperceptibly into the face, and does not have a hard edge where it finishes.

10 · Summary of straight make-up

In the foregoing chapters we have seen how to colour a face, shade it for lighting, and shade and highlight it to change the structure. We have defined the eyes and eyebrows and coloured the mouth. We have, in fact, covered all that is necessary to achieve our first objective – to make the performer's face look right to the audience in the context of the production and its design, and in the theatre in which it is being performed. This includes, of course, regularising or adjusting the face to make it ideal or to accentuate some feature to aid the characterisation.

We have not discussed making-up hands, which is a frequent cause of dissension. In all branches of the theatre except for ballet the hands should be painted one or two shades paler than the face. A natural hand is, almost without exception, paler than the face of its owner. Pancake, or one of the transparent body tints mentioned in chapter 17 is the best to use, as it is less likely to rub off on to costumes than one of the other liquid types of body make-up. In ballet, except in special cases, the hands are not made up, as they would mark the partner's costume.

Ballet make-up

This is nearly always heavier and more extreme than a normal straight make-up, partly because ballet is frequently performed in large theatres and opera houses, and partly because there has always been a tradition of fantasy in ballet, which still carries on its effect on make-up, even in the realistic ballets of today. Mainly it is a question of slightly brighter-coloured foundations, stronger eye and eyebrow shading, and considerably heavier eye lining and eyebrows. Female dancers usually wear longer and thicker artificial eyelashes than their actress counterparts.

Opera

Singers, usually with reason, tend to make more use of shading than actors and actresses, mainly due to the fact mentioned earlier that the best voices tend to come from the roundest faces. This shading is apt to be overdone, and one can frequently see singers painted to resemble masks, which is no aid to characterisation or to intelligent use of facial expression. Eyes and eyebrows need stronger definition in opera for the same reason as in ballet – large theatres, intense lighting, and large numbers of people crowded together on the stage.

Musicals

Make-up for musicals in large theatres has most of the characteristics of make-up for ballet, especially with regard to the colouring; but eyes and eyebrows are not usually painted as heavily. In smaller theatres the same amount of eye and eyebrow make-up is used as in a straight play, but the brighter coloured foundations are still adhered to, giving a slightly artificial effect of healthiness and well-being.

Some male performers tend to use a cabaret or revue style of make-up in musicals, which is apt to give a blank look to their face, with practically no eyes, eyebrows or mouth.

Revue and cabaret

These have exactly the opposite performing conditions to opera and ballet – close proximity of the audience, an intimate style of presentation, and frequently soft, diffused lighting. The basic rule is, the closer the public, the lighter the make-up (in detail, not necessarily in colour). Pancake or Pan-stick, very lightly applied, are ideal, and very subtle eye and eyebrow make-up is essential for men, although women may wear almost as much as a ballerina without seeming out of place.

11 · Character make-up

This is a general term that usually covers everything other than straight make-up. I prefer to keep stylised and fantastic make-up in separate categories and include only the varied forms of naturalistic make-up under the heading of character. These forms include various ways of ageing the face, of changing the performer's character, and all the different varieties of racial make-up. Frequently the forms overlap – a young actor may have to appear as an ageing villain, or a middle-aged Englishman as a very old Chinaman. In the following chapters we discuss ageing and altering the face and various examples of racial make-up, and these can be combined as required.

For age and character types it is well worthwhile to study the works of the great painters, either in the nearest art gallery or in reproduction. Franz Hals and Rembrandt, to name only two, painted superb examples of facial types, and the technique of painting the characterisation shows clearly on the canvas. One can see the placing of the shading and the highlights, and the technique of painting in the eyes and eyebrows. The first time that I appeared as a Negro on the stage (in the ballet *Scheherazade*) I was greatly helped in my make-up by a painting of a Moor by James Northcote, which was at that time hanging in the Manchester Art Gallery.

With racial types, it is a help to study photographs of the race that one is trying to simulate. Magazines and newspaper colour supplements provide examples of most races in the world, even if only in the advertisements. With global travel becoming more common, one has also the opportunity to study many races in the flesh. All large cities have an influx of foreigners in the tourist season, and one can study many races without leaving home.

Adapting or changing the face
With character make-up one can adapt one's face to the type required, or one can completely alter it and change it into something quite different. The first course is undoubtedly the best to follow, especially in small and medium-sized theatres. A make-up that is painted against the structure of the face may look convincing in repose, but it will distort with speaking or singing, and with changes of expression. In a large theatre or an opera house the make-up can be exaggerated and the distortions are not apparent, but this is not possible in a smaller theatre. Fortunately most races contain a variety of types, and one can choose the type that is closest to one's own face. There are, for example, Japanese with high noses and long faces, as well as ones with round faces and snub noses. There are round-faced Spaniards as well as the aquiline type that immediately comes to mind. There are Negroes with high noses, Arabs with small noses – in fact, a great variety in every race. By finding a type close to your own appearance, and making-up to that type, one can achieve something that looks real on the stage, and not just a fine example of make-up.

In ageing or characterisation, the same rules apply. An aged version of your own face will look more real than a complex of shadows cutting across the natural muscles, and a villainous version of yourself will carry better than a villainous mask painted against the facial structure. In any naturalistic make-up, the audience should think how right the performer looks in the role – not what a wonderful make-up he or she is wearing.

12 · Different age groups

In the previous chapters we have discussed the techniques of shading and highlighting, and how to alter the structure of the various features as required. We shall now see how these techniques can be used for altering the age group of the face.

Ageing the face
The most common use is ageing the face, an effect which, to many performers, means painting as many thin lines and highlights as possible on to an otherwise young face, and leaving it at that.

For a successful ageing make-up, it is essential to discover how an old or ageing face differs from the face of a young person. When one is young, the facial tissues are firm, and the contours of the face are inclined to be rounded, like a fresh apple or peach. As one ages, two things happen: the tissues lose their fullness and firmness, allowing the skin to fall more loosely over the bone structure, which therefore shows more clearly, and the habitual expression of the face develops the facial muscles and makes a distortion of the original face. The face that was fresh and firm has become loose, possibly sagging, and what was a passing expression has become a fixed part of the facial structure. If one looks at the faces about one in everyday life, it is often possible to see how they will develop in twenty or thirty years – the future is plainly written on them. The fresh colour of youth also changes, becoming more yellow or parchment-coloured, or the opposite – a deeper and rather more red colour verging on purple, especially on fat faces. With very white hair, one sometimes gets a pale pink tone to the skin.

To achieve this with make-up, one must first study one's facial structure, and see where the rot will set in. Firstly the colour. With a thin person the tendency is to become sallower. Mixing a little Leichner No. 5 and possibly a little of a light brown liner with a normal cream or grease foundation achieves this easily. With Pancake or Panstik, Natural Beige gives a sallow tone to mens' skin, and Ivory a very old parchment colour. Pale Flesh (085) gives a very pale pinkish tone. For a woman, one must decide whether she would be wearing make-up normally or not. If she is, the colour is not very important, though a shade or two paler than usual will stress the age. A woman wanting to look as if she was wearing no make-up could use Pale Flesh (085) or Ivory for an old parchment look. 21 is very good for pink and white old ladies.

For plump or fat people, the tendency is to become more florid. No. 8 or 9 mixed with the normal cream or grease foundation, and carmine 3 or lake added to the cheek colour, will achieve this. I do not care for Pancake for a florid make-up, as it seems to me to lack the fullness required, but if you use it, choose a colour one shade darker than your normal foundation, and use more and brighter cheek colour than in your straight make-up.

As mentioned in chapter 9, the jawline is one of the first places to show the approach of age. The jowls tend to sag, and an inverted 'V'-shape appears under each side of the mouth. The indentation from the nostrils to the mouth becomes heavier, and can be shaded in, with a corresponding highlight on the fold of flesh beside it (FIG 32). The hollows around the eyes become more pronounced on a thin face (see chapter 4) and also the shadows beneath the cheekbones, which should be accentuated with shading and a corresponding highlight on the actual cheekbone (FIG 32). This last, of course, does not apply to fat faces, where the fullness of the cheek sags, and the jowls become more prominent (FIG 33). Some fat faces, however, retain their roundness well into old age, becoming more brightly coloured and needing only a highlighting on the lower part of the cheek, emphasising of the double chins, and the usual inverted 'V'-shaped indentation below the ends of the mouth (FIG 34).

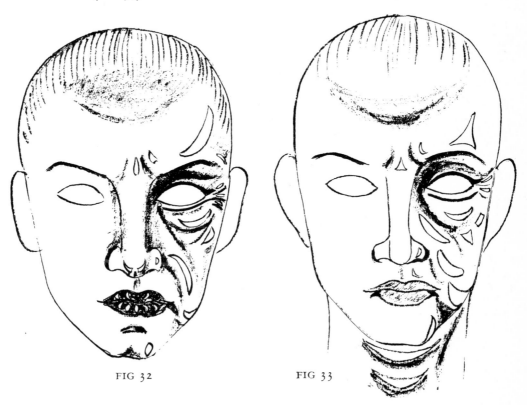

FIG 32   FIG 33

The nose becomes either more pinched with age (usually on thin faces) or in some cases larger and more florid. For the first, shadow the indentation round the nostrils, and lightly shadow the sides of the nose, making the shadow heavier each side of the bridge of the nose, and joining it in with the shadow under the eyebrow, which can be heavier than usual, possibly with some brown mixed with the No. 8 or 9. A touch of shadow inside the nostrils helps the pinched look, and a small sharp highlight on the tip of the nose, and on the edge of the nostrils, will emphasise it further. A more florid nose is achieved with colouring – mixing some No. 8 or 9 with the foundation, and following with a little carmine 2, 3, or lake, depending on how deep a colour is wanted. No shading should be used, but a touch of highlight on either side of the tip of the nose and on the sides of the nostrils will help to enlarge the nose. With a Pancake foundation, apply Max Factor Dark Red (4) Moist Rouge (or Leichner carmine 2, 3, or lake) before applying the foundation.

With a thin or a sagging fat face, the hollows below the eyes become accentuated and there are frequently bags beneath the eyes. On a thin face,

71

a diagonal shadow from the inside corner of the eye, down and across the cheek, ages the face considerably. A further shadow starting just outside the eye, and coming diagonally down and across to join the first shadow immediately below the eye, about an inch down from it, will give the foundation of a convincing bag beneath the eye (FIG 32). This can be accentuated by a heavier line drawn in a darker colour around the actual shape of the bag, with a corresponding highlight inside it.

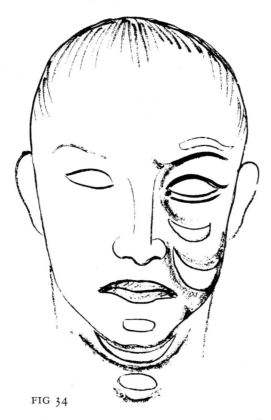

FIG 34

Two or three wrinkles can be painted radiating outwards from the corner of the eye (FIG 32), but take care that they are painted as described in chapter 6, and are not just thin lines with no meaning or carrying power.

The temples become slightly sunken with advancing age, and the shape of the skull shows through more clearly. They should be shaded, with the weight of the shadow at the front next to the edge of the bone, which should be highlighted (FIG 32).

Wrinkles on the forehead do not carry well, unless a very detailed wrinkled face is being painted for a small theatre. If they are used, they should follow the lines of the natural wrinkles (perhaps missing one of these out, to avoid overcrowding) and should be painted as described in chapter 6. A more natural effect for the stage is a broad 'V'-shaped shadow in the centre of the forehead, with corresponding highlights above the eyebrows, which may be linked with the highlights beside the temples (FIG 32). This carries well, and gives the effect of the skull showing through the ageing tissues. Two horizontal shadows up from the bridge of the nose, with corresponding highlights (FIG 32), complete the ageing of the forehead.

The eyes of older people are less bright than in youth, so the eyelines should be either painted in grey, or painted more lightly than usual in black or brown. The eyelashes should be painted with grey mascara or, with a white wig, brushed with white greasepaint, which gives a faded look to the eye. The eyelid shadow should be brown or grey, except with florid types, when it can be in lake. No white dot should be used in the outer corner of the eye, and in quite old make-up, no red dot in the inner corner. There are suggestions in chapter 5 for white and grey eyebrows, and various methods of ageing the mouth are discussed in chapter 8.

From these various suggestions, choose those that apply to your own face and the face that you want to achieve. The structure of the face can be altered, as well as aged, by using the techniques described in chapter 6, and details of character (small eyes, loose mouth, etc.) from the chapters on the separate features. Wigs, moustaches, etc., are discussed in chapter 16.

Making faces younger

To make a face younger one reverses the previous process, and removes as much incidental detail as possible from the face. A Pancake foundation is very suitable for this, as it tends to flatten the structure and blot out detail. A youthful colour should be chosen – peach shades rather than pink for women, and tan shades for men. The colours given in the chart for straight make-up in chapter 2 are suitable.

To give an effect of exaggerated or artificial youthfulness, such as an ageing star determined to appear young, or a perpetual male juvenile, a man can use Florid Male (2879) Pancake.

For a youthful look, the face should have the normal colouring on the cheeks and under the eyebrows, and the eyes and eyebrows should be painted fairly strongly, and very clearly – any smudging will detract from the freshness that is required. The plainer and more straightforward the make-up, the more successful it will be.

Adults as children

Children's faces are less formed than adults', and I have always found that the less make-up that adults wear when they are playing children, the better. If the lighting is straightforward, the best answer is usually no make-up at all. In a large theatre, women may wear their normal street make-up (unless they normally wear an exaggerated eye make-up) with a lighter coloured lipstick than usual. For men, if the lighting distorts the natural skin colour too much, a light foundation of Panstik or Pancake in a normal youthful colour can be worn, with mascara only on the eyelashes (no eye lines) and a slight darkening of the natural eyebrow. A minimum of cheek colour is required, with no shading under the eyebrows and only a very light touch of violet on the eyelids. The mouth should be painted with Max Factor Brown Red (9) Moist Rouge.

Children, and children as adults

The less that is done to a child's face on the stage, the better. A light Panstick foundation (in the paler of the shades given for their colouring in chapter 2) with the minimum of cheek colour, and very little colour under the eyebrows and on the eyelids (violet), gives the best effect. Eye lines should be avoided – just mascara on the lashes and the natural eyebrows brushed lightly with mascara should be enough. For boys, Max Factor Brown Red (9) Moist Rouge should be used for the mouth, and for girls Leichner No. 9 greasepaint with a small addition of carmine 2 or 3.

For children playing adults, a little more make-up is required – slightly more colour on the cheeks and under the eyebrows, and stronger colour on the lips and possibly the eyelids. For girls, the eyes can be painted in with a very light version of the normal eye lines, but for boys just a line above the eye should be sufficient. Eyebrows can be lightly pencilled in, but anything at all heavy will look unnatural on a child's face.

The importance of hand make-up

All ageing make-up must be balanced by an equivalent make-up of the hands and any visible part of the body. If the neck is exposed, it should be made up with a slightly exaggerated form of the technique for slimming the neck described in chapter 9, except for fat people, who should emphasise any double chins with highlights and shadows. The hands should be painted in a shade corresponding to the face, but one or two shades lighter (a Pancake or a liquid body tint is best) and shadows should be painted in the gaps between the fingers and carried on to the back of the hand. The knuckles should have a highlight on each of them, and the sinews on the back of the hand should be picked out with a highlight (FIG 35). One will then avoid having a smooth young hand with a wrinkled old face. With a plump ageing facial make-up the hands present less difficulty, but they should be painted one or two shades lighter than the face, and the knuckles picked out with highlight.

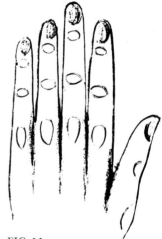

FIG 35

13 · Racial make-up

In chapter 11 we discussed the advantages of choosing the nearest equivalent to one's own face for a racial type, rather than trying to paint too much against the natural structure. The extreme effects of make-up achieved by the great actors in the early days of this century were lit either by gaslight, or by very primitive electric lighting, and they would look ludicrous on a stage with modern lighting. Our effects nowadays must be much more subtle and realistic if they are to convince the public, and this eliminates elaborate alteration of the facial structure in any but the largest theatres.

Scandinavian and northern European

This is more a question of colouring than of structure. Scandinavians, Dutch, and to a lesser extent, Germans, are always expected to be blonde, although a visit to any of these countries reveals a great number of brunettes. Blonde wigs (or naturally blonde performers) with brown eyebrows and eye lining go a long way to achieve the desired effect. Scandinavians do not, however, have pale skins. They stay a golden tan all summer and most of the winter (aided by a great deal of ski-ing) and this should be simulated by using either the darker shades suggested in chapter 2 for fair performers, or by mixing a little Leichner No. 8 and dark brown liner into the normal cream or grease foundation. Use Max Factor Translucent (c3–238) powder. Swedes in particular tend to have very regular features, which can be simulated by a very light shading of the nose, and a corrective shading to any structural irregularities. The Dutch frequently have very wide faces, particularly at the widest point of the jawbone. This can be simulated by a highlight on the widest part of the jaw, and the tipped up nose so often seen in Holland can be achieved by a triangular shading on the tip of the nose with a quite strong highlight above it.

Mediterranean

This is again largely a question of colour. Mediterranean races have olive skins (not orange, as one frequently sees on the stage) with clearly defined eyes and eyebrows, and usually dark hair. When the hair is fair or auburn, it is usually thicker and crisper than the hair of people in cooler climates.

An effective olive shade can be achieved by mixing Leichner No. 8 and dark brown liner into a No. 30 Satin Smooth foundation, and adding a very little Leichner No. 3 green. This will prevent any hint of the painted orange colour which looks so artificial. Adding the same colours to your normal greasepaint foundation will achieve the same effect; or one can use Leichner No. 6½ (if you possess it) with some additional No. 8. Women, of course, do not need so much of these colours, and they should add them to their normal foundation colour. Both sexes can powder with Max Factor Translucent (c3–238). For Pancake, women can use the colour called Oriental (B.M.) and men c.t.v.9w, 10w, 11w, or 12w. For a less olive tan, women can wear Light Olive Tan (k.6) and men Latin (k.f.8). All these colours, except Oriental (B.M.) are also available in Panstik. The Pancake colours can be used as hand or body make-up, or one can use Body Tint Clear.

The eyebrows should be strongly drawn in black (except for an actual blonde, who is unlikely to look convincingly Mediterranean without a wig) and the eyes should be outlined (again in black) rather more strongly than in a straight make-up. The red dot in the inner corner of the eye should be slightly more pronounced, and a white dot at the outside corner of the eye can be worn even in small theatres. In large theatres, a white dot under the inside white of the eye can be worn, but do not carry it all the way along under the eye, or you may look as if you are going to have a fit. The mouth should be more strongly coloured than in a straight make-up, using more carmine 3 on the upper lip and carmine 2 on the lower. The cheek colour need not be any stronger than in a straight make-up. For a peasant make-up, a horizontal highlight above the bridge of the nose gives a slightly primitive effect (FIG 36).

FIG 36

Middle Eastern

Members of the Arab races range in colour from a darker version of Mediterranean to a very dark, greenish brown, and mostly have very pronounced features. Popular fancy always pictures Arabs as hawk-nosed and hawk-eyed, even if they are dressed in lounge suits and occupied with mundane business matters. If they are galloping over the sands of the desert (*Desert Song*, etc.) then no fantasy is too extreme. Here is one of the ideal occasions for using nose putty, and for painting striking black eyebrows and intense burning eyes. The colouring can be achieved as for a Mediterranean race –

75

No. 8 dark brown liner and No. 3 green added to the normal foundation –
but the overall effect can be slightly darker. For Pancake or Panstik, Light
Egyptian for women and Dark Egyptian for men are the most suitable.
These may also be used for body make-up, or Max Factor Body Tint
Dark Tan (265) or Dark Olive Brown (273), if a transparent colour is
preferred. Very little cheek colour should be used for men, and the lips
should have a very little lake added to the basic No. 8. The eyes and eyebrows
are drawn strongly in black, and women can wear a great deal of coloured
eye-shadow and a very heavy eye make-up. Women can also wear a fairly
bright cheek colour and an obviously made-up mouth, to match the heavy
make-up of the eyes.

Indian

India is a sub-continent, and contains many races and types with a wide
range of colour and features. The features may be smooth and unobtrusive,
or strongly aquiline. As a rough generalisation, the more aquiline types tend
to be darker than those with smaller features. The eyes are usually strongly
outlined with black lashes, and the eyebrows, which are clearly defined, tend
to be thicker than those of Europeans. Adding No. 8, dark brown liner and
either carmine No. 3 or No. 3 green (depending if a warm or an olive tone is
required) to the normal foundation gives a satisfactory colour. Powder with
Max Factor Translucent Powder. In Pancake or Panstik the colour called
Light Indian (T.D.4) is ideal for men or women. For darker shades use
Dark Indian (665-R) and for paler shades for women use Shader (A.L.).
This last is also very suitable for Eurasians. Any of these Pancake colours
can be used for body make-up, or Body Tint Medium Golden Tan (264) or
Dark Tan (265). Indian women traditionally wear a large amount of eye
make-up and coloured eyeshadow. For women a fair amount of cheek
colour is suitable, but not for men. The lips should be fairly full and rather
dark – for men a touch of lake and brown added to the basic No. 8, and for
women obviously painted, with a generous use of carmine 3. Hindu women
wear a caste mark on their forehead, the one most frequently seen on Indians
in Europe being a red dot about half an inch in diameter immediately
above the nose. Pressing a stick of carmine 2 or 3 against the forehead
achieves this very simply.

Oriental

The only oriental types that we shall discuss are Chinese and Japanese, which
have a great deal in common facially. More subtle variations on the eastern
face, such as Koreans or Mongolians, do not mean very much to a western
audience, and it is doubtful if the differences could be clearly shown in make-
up on a European face.

   The over-riding feature of Oriental faces is their smoothness of structure.
Even the aquiline type of Japanese have a smooth, rounded face and their
noses, although high, are not in any way angular. A perfectly flat Pancake
foundation is the best method to achieve this look on a European face – it
blots out a great deal of the structural detail, which gets us a long way
towards our objective. In opera and operetta (*Madame Butterfly*, *The Mikado*,
The Land of Smiles) I have always used 24 Pancake for women and 26 Pancake
for men. Alternatively one could use Oriental (B.M.) or Natural Beige for
women and Chinese or Mikado for men. For a more realistic make-up,

and for peasants, for Chinese use the Pancake called Chinese, and for Japanese use Light Indian (T.D.4), applied thinly. Women need only a little cheek colour, and men none at all. On a rounded or flat face no shading or highlighting is needed, but on a face with strong features the recess between the eyes and the eyebrows should be highlighted by being painted with white lining (or Leichner No 1) and powdered with talc before the Pancake is applied. No shadow should be worn under the eyebrows or on the eye-lids. This helps to give the smooth look round the eyes so characteristic of Orientals.

The outstanding thing about Chinese and Japanese eyes is not that they slope up (a great number of them do not) but that they mostly are quite literally almond-shaped, with a strong upward curve to the upper line of the eye in by the nose, and a smooth slope out to the end of the eye. Many Japanese eyes have almost a look of sloping downward, as the widest part of the eyes is in by the nose. Chinese eyes have more of a tendency to slope upwards, but they still have the widest part of the eye set well in. This is, of course, a generalisation; there are so many different types of Chinese and Japanese that no one rule could possibly cover them all. The eyebrows again do not slope particularly more than those of Europeans, but having gone up, they cut off short and do not come down again. Many Japanese eyebrows start fairly high and come out and slightly down, again cutting off short.

FIG 37   FIG 38   FIG 39

FIG 37 shows a suggested eye make-up for a Japanese and FIG 38 a Chinese. Notice that the upper eyeline is carried down to meet the lower line at the inside of the eye, accentuating the high curve of that part of the eye. When making up for their theatre, both races accentuate the eyes and the eyebrow structure. Plate 24 shows a classical Chinese make-up (described in chapter 14), with an interesting way of painting the eye, shown in figure 38. This is not particularly easy on a European face, as we tend to have more curve to the eyelid, but with practice it can be achieved, looking most effective in a large theatre. Japanese women in a traditional make-up paint their eyebrows almost right out, and leave only about an inch of fairly thick eyebrow close to the bridge of the nose. Although traditional, to our eyes this is apt to look rather funny, and it should only be used in the western theatre in a comedy or grotesque role.

The mouth should be rather shorter and fuller than usual, particularly for Japanese. Paint out the ends of the mouth with the Pancake foundation, and paint short rounded lips, using No. 8 with a little carmine 3 for men and carmine 2 or 3 for women.

Negro make-up

Amongst the Negro races there is a wide range of colour and facial structure, giving one ample opportunity to choose a type similar to one's own faci structure. Most Negroes have wide nostrils, full, rather prominent mouths and large dark eyes. By using an appropriate colour and emphasising these features, a convincing effect can usually be obtained.

For the occasional Negro make-up, in order to avoid buying special make-up, I have always used Satin Smooth No. 30 as a base, and added Leichner No. 8, carmine 3, dark brown liner and a very little black. The No. 8 and the carmine 3 are essential to prevent a grey look under stage lighting. The same effect can be achieved by adding these colours to a normal greasepaint foundation, or one can use No. 8, No. 11 and a little carmine 3. Negro No. 2 Panstik is a good colour if one wants to buy a base specially, but the best technique I know for a Negro make-up was devised by Douglas Young of the Max Factor London Salon. This uses Pancake Negro No. 2, applied with a sponge dampened with Dark Olive Brown (273) Body Tint (instead of water), and it gives a perfect colour and skin texture (pl 1). Shadows are painted in over the foundation with black Pancake, and highlights are achieved by lightly rubbing off the foundation with a piece of cotton wool dampened with the body tint, so that the natural colour shows through. One can modify this technique of highlighting for use with grease and cream make-up (rubbing very lightly at the required areas of the foundation with dry cotton wool), as a highlight painted on a very dark foundation is rarely successful. For a paler skinned Negro or Negress one can use Negro No. 1 Pancake. No colour is needed on the cheeks or under the eyebrow. The nostrils can be widened by highlighting the widest point and shading inside the nostril, and, in a large theatre, by drawing a curving shadow about a quarter of an inch from the outside of the nostril and highlighting between the shadow and the actual nostril, also shading inside the curve of the nostril (FIG 40). The mouth should be outlined with white lining colour outside the rim of the natural shape, and then have the Pancake foundation painted right over it. A black shadow should then be painted right around the highlighted area, with a stronger shadow beneath the mouth (FIG 40). This will give a large, rather protruding mouth, in very much the right colour. If a redder effect is desired, use Max Factor Dark Brown Red (9) Moist Rouge on the mouth before applying the Pancake.

FIG 40

The eyes should be heavily outlined in black, with a strong white triangle at the outer corner and heavy mascara on the upper lashes. For his celebrated interpretation of Othello, Sir Lawrence Olivier wore short, thick eyelashes to accentuate the eye, and painted white along the edge of the lower eyelid, inside the lashes (pl 6).

This emphasising of the eye, nostrils and mouth should give a sufficiently Negroid look to most faces, and by observation one will discover effects of highlighting and shading that will enhance the effect on one's own face. The hands and visible parts of the body should be painted as described in chapter 17.

14 · Stylised make-up

This is a term that is rather hard to define exactly. It ranges from a mannered exaggeration of nature to the beginnings of fantastic make-up, and takes in many things by the way. Broadly speaking, a stylised make-up is used where the overall style and design of a production take precedence over the individual characteristics of a performer or a characterisation.

Oriental theatre
The traditional Chinese and Japanese theatres are an extreme example of stylisation. The performers wear a traditional make-up with clearly defined rules of shape and colour, and the audience can tell from the make-up what kind of character the performer represents. These traditions have built up over a very long period of time, and some of the examples (which could more properly perhaps be called fantastic rather than stylised) are most effective (pls 22, 23). They are only of academic interest to performers in the western theatre, except for the rare occasion when a play or opera is performed in an approximation of the traditional Oriental manner. Usually when this is done, the designer will create his own make-up for each character, rather than trying to rely on the authentic Oriental version, and the performer should copy the design as closely as possible, using the nearest colour available in make-up. It is surprising the large variety of actual colours (apart from flesh tonings) available in make-up. Both Max Factor and Leichner provide nearly every colour one could need. Max Factor in Pancake and Panstiks, and Leichner in greasepaint sticks and liners, as well as Spotlite Klear. Any colour not available in these can be found in Max Factor lining colours and Leichner eyeshadow. An unusual range of colours is made in a German range of make-up called Kryolan, which is now obtainable in England.

The easiest of the traditional Oriental faces to achieve is the Chinese make-up for a young woman (pl 24). The face is painted with Leichner No. 1½ as a foundation, and then a heavy shading of carmine 3 is applied between the eye and the eyebrow and carried down both sides of the nose, under the eye, and down the sides of the cheeks, fading out towards the chin. The strongest area of colour is between the eye and the eyebrow. This make-up is not powdered, but if it appears too greasy, it can be lightly dusted with talc. An alternative foundation is white Pancake, which is applied over the carmine shading, which may then be strengthened with dry rouge if necessary. The eyes and eyebrows are drawn as described in chapter 13 (FIG 39), and the mouth is painted quite heavily in carmine 3 and can be outlined in black.

Clown make-up
This is the most usual form of stylised make-up in the western world, and it is divided into white-faced clowns and others. The white-faced clowns are either smart and sophisticated with a strong vein of fantasy (pl 46), or pathetic, in the Pierrot tradition. In either case they are based on an overall white foundation, which can be white greasepaint, white Pancake, Panstick or Max Factor Clown White, which gives the best overall dead white effect. Many clown faces stop dead at the chin-line, leaving the neck in its natural colour, but some carry the white on down to the costume line.

The natural eyebrows are painted out; they may be stuck down or merely painted over as desired, depending on whether they are bushy or fairly flat, and on for what size of theatre the make-up is intended. No shading is used at all, and any colour on the cheeks is usually painted in a clear geometrical shape, such as a circle or a triangle, sometimes with a different shape on each cheek, and usually outlined with black. The eyebrows are painted in black with a fantastic expression, such as two inverted 'V' shapes, or two half circles, and occasionally a different shape for each eyebrow. The eyes are painted as dots or vertical lozengers, or any shape that appeals, again in black; and any colour on the eyelid is painted in a strong bright shade such as green, blue or strong violet, in a shape that balances the eye and eyebrow. The mouth on a white-faced clown is usually small, neat, and clearly defined, with a slight exaggeration such as two strong points in the centre of the upper lip, and one on the lower, and is generally in a clear red with a black outline.

Pierrots use no colour on the face except for heavy blue or green between the eye and the eyebrows. The eyebrows are in the traditional shape, and the eyes slope downwards (FIG 41). The mouth is usually dark (carmine 3 or lake) and is sometimes painted to turn down at the corners.

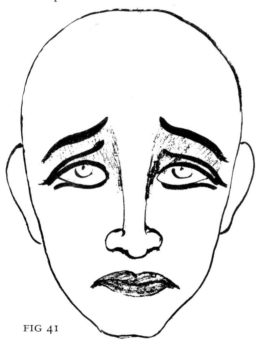

FIG 41

Clowns, other than white-faced, usually wear a fairly strongly coloured foundation – a deep tan (Max Factor 30 or 31 Satin Smooth or Pancake) or a rich flesh (Leichner No. 8 or 9 with very little Lit K or No. 5 added). The make-up is usually comic, with enormous mouths painted either in red or white, frequently turning down at the ends, and huge surprised eyebrows, often in large inverted 'U' shapes. These are sometimes filled into the eyes with white or a bright colour, and a distorted eye – a star or a triangle – painted up into them. The cheeks may be left the colour of the foundation, or have a bright geometrical shape painted on to them. Most clowns of this type either paint their nose red, or wear a large false nose of the type bought at joke shops.

Formal ritualistic make-up

This usually appears in present-day theatre only in plays and operas dealing with Egypt and the early eastern Mediterranean civilisations – *Cleopatra* and *Samson and Delilah* for example – where characters must look as if they are wearing a heavy formal make-up. This is harder than it might at first appear, especially in large theatres, as the effect of the make-up is not only diminished by lighting and distance, but the heavy exotic wigs and head-dresses associated with the period also tend to overwhelm the details of the face. An example of this is shown in the photographs of Maureen Guy as Delilah in the Sadler's Wells production of *Samson and Delilah* designed by Ralph Koltai (pls 14, 16). In close-up the make-up seems grotesquely heavy, but in the photograph taken from a medium distance, it already looks almost naturalistic. The eye lining and the eyebrows for this type of make-up should be painted in the most intense black possible – a liquid black eyeliner, black Pancake, Max Factor black eye lining or black greasepaint. An eyebrow pencil is not sufficient for the intensity required. The eyeshadow should be a strong clear colour, with no pretensions to naturalness, or a metallic paint – gold or silver. The lining should be as clear and precise as possible, and the mouth should be outlined in black.

Examples of western stylised make-up

The photograph of Sir Laurence Olivier as Coriolanus (pl 8) gives a fine example of a straightforward stylised make-up. The exaggerated painting of the mouth, eyes and eyebrows made the face fit exactly into the overall stylised design of the production.

In Pizzetti's opera *Murder in the Cathedral* (based on T. S. Eliot's play) at Sadler's Wells – directed by Basil Coleman and designed by Ralph Koltai – the female chorus were built into the stylised setting as statues on the façade of the cathedral. The costumes and head-dresses were stone-coloured, so it was necessary for the faces and hands of the chorus to be stone-coloured also. This was achieved by painting both the faces and the hands with a Max Factor Pancake which exactly matched the colour of the costume, and using Leichner No. 9 on the lips and under the eyebrows, with no colour on the cheeks. The eyes and eyebrows were drawn in with black. The final effect was of statuesque figures in all over stone colour, not distorted or grotesque in any way. In the same production no make-up at all was used for the faces of the male chorus, who appeared as monks. The aim was to give an effect of anonymous groups of people; and with the wigs all the same design and a lack of detail in the monks' faces, the chorus appeared as a solid entity and not as a group of individuals.

A further development of this was used in Glen Byam Shaw's production of Stravinsky's opera *The Rake's Progress*, designed by Motley. The lunatics in the Madhouse Scene were dressed in rags, and wore no foundation but shaded the structure of their faces with light brown, brown, grey and green, painted straight on to the skin. No other colour was used, and the eyes and eyebrows were either left unpainted, or roughly painted in with black. This gave an impression of rotting flesh, with here and there some burning, staring eyes.

It can be seen from these examples that stylised make-up must be planned in close relationship with the designer, or it has no meaning. The whole intention is to carry the director's and the designer's style on to the performer's face, so that it fits exactly into the overall pattern.

15 · Fantastic make-up

Fantastic make-up is generally more extreme than stylised make-up, and it has a different intention. Where a stylised make-up either makes the face carry on the style of the sets and costumes, or is in a firmly set tradition, a fantastic make-up is primarily concerned with the effect that it creates by itself, and knows no bounds except those set by the area of the face – it may have no relationship with the actual structure of the face. It is used for super-natural creatures – monsters and demons – and many of the unusual creatures met with in opera and ballet – serpents played by dancers, and some of the odder creatures at the bottom of the Rhine.

Even more than with stylised make-up, it is essential to work with the designer. Mostly the type of make-up required is indicated in the costume design, and if this does not show it sufficiently clearly, the designer will usually oblige with a sketch of the face as he sees it. It is then up to the performer to make this work as make-up. When Picasso designed the de Falla–Massine ballet *Le Chapeau Tricorne* for the Diaghileff Ballet Russe in 1919, he invented some extreme effects of make-up for the dancers and actually painted them on to their astonished faces to judge the initial effect. Not many designers nowadays have either the desire or the ability to do this.

Painting a fantastic make-up
One must first decide whether the make-up is basically on a foundation of a single colour, or whether it is in areas of different colour. In the first case, paint the whole face with the required foundation colour – usually a flesh colour, or green, yellow or red, all easily acquired in standard make-up – and then paint the other colours and shadings over the foundation. Powder, and continue with lining. Most make-up in odd colours presents a problem with powdering, and a good solution is Max Factor Translucent (c3–238) powder, or even talc, which will bleach the colours slightly. If it is a face that can be left shiny, leave well alone and do not powder it, but be careful not to brush against it, or it will wipe off. Using coloured Pancake, which needs no powdering, is a solution to a clear coloured matt surface.

If the colour is in separate areas, paint each area in the colour desired, fading the colours together where they meet, or keeping a clear line between, whichever is indicated in the design. If a very firm line is needed between separate areas of colour, paint a black line as a divide, using either black greasepaint or black lining colour and a brush.

When painting abstract coloured sections on to a face, always check from the side, using two mirrors, as well as from the front. A human face is not flat, and what appears as a circle or triangle from the front may appear as something quite different from the side, or from three-quarter face. One must adjust, so that from all angles the result is as close as possible to the original intention. Odd coloured shapes, such as zig-zag eyebrows in bright green, always need outlining in black to make them carry. Make sure that the design on the face is bold enough to show to the audience and does not come over as a meaningless mess of different colours and shapes.

16 · Use of putty, wigs and false hair

Nose putty is a great help in all exaggerated make-up, and can also be used with subtlety in character make-up. As the name suggests, it is used principally on the nose, but in exaggerated forms of make-up may also be used on the chin and cheekbones, where it must be firmly attached with spirit gum, or it will become loose with the action of the muscles. Both Max Factor and Leichner make nose putty, which comes in short sticks and is very hard when bought – Max Factor generally being slightly softer than Leichner. It must be softened by being worked in the hands until it has a texture like plasticine. It is advisable to allow some time for this the first time that the putty is used, as it can be quite a lengthy process. Fortunately one can use the same putty a number of times, and if there is not too great an interval between the uses it should remain fairly malleable.

Technique of using nose putty

It is advisable to stick the putty on with spirit gum, which is also supplied by both Max Factor and Leichner. It is possible when using small amounts of fairly new putty to get a good adhesion without spirit gum, but there is always the risk of its working loose in performance.

The putty is applied before the foundation. Having got it to a sufficient stage of malleability, take the amount needed (always less than one expects) and mould it roughly to the desired shape, holding it against the nose to judge the amount and shape required. Paint spirit gum on to the area of skin where the putty is to be applied (it will sting, which is quite normal) and allow it to become tacky. Press the prepared piece of putty firmly into place, and hold it for a few seconds to make sure that it has adhered. Using the fingers of both hands, to ensure that the pressure is even from both sides, mould the putty into the shape required. Take care that the edges of the putty blend fairly imperceptibly into the surrounding skin and that the putty does not have an abrupt edge. This can be facilitated by dipping the fingers in cold cream or oil, to smooth over the junction of the putty and the skin. Check the shape and size of the addition with two mirrors, making sure that the profile and the half profile have the shape that you desire. Paint the foundation over the entire face, putty and all, and then continue with the make-up in the normal way. I find a Satin Smooth foundation the easiest to apply over a nose putty, but performers generally use their normal foundation.

Uses of putty

Putty can be used to make an enormous nose for a witch or a monster, or to build up a retroussé nose to a straight one. A small dab below the bridge of the nose will make a normal nose into a Roman profile (FIG 42), or smaller amount on the bridge of the nose will make it appear Grecian (FIG 43). Many snub-nosed performers habitually build an aquiline nose to add distinction to their profile.

Chins may have an addition to the point, but only in an exaggerated make-up, as it is almost impossible to make this look natural. An exaggerated make-up can also have high cheekbones added in putty, or a heavy bulge added to the brow, but I would hesitate to advise this for a naturalistic

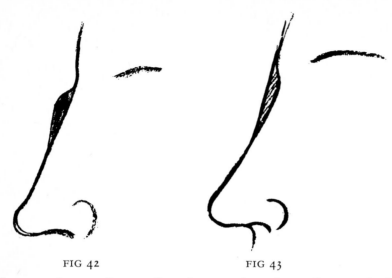

FIG 42   FIG 43

make-up, or in a small or medium theatre, where these effects can be better achieved by skilful use of highlighting.

Performers who have a feature that needs constant correction for a straight make-up, such as a nose that is too deeply retroussé, can have plastic shapes made which can be easily and quickly applied, without the trouble of moulding them for each performance. One shape can be used several times, which makes them reasonably economic. Unfortunately, very few firms make these plastic shapes, as the fact that they have to be specially moulded for each person makes them a bad commercial proposition. A firm or individual who specialises in plastic work for the theatre (armour, properties and so on) will often oblige by making a supply of the shape required by the performer.

Wigs

These are made by specialists, and bought or hired for use in the theatre. They have become increasingly natural in recent times, and equally increasingly fragile, and must be treated with great care. The old tough type of theatrical wig, with a heavy forehead piece and solid bands of wefted hair (apt to look like a tea-cosy) has been replaced by a light knotted hair wig, usually with net edges, which does not stand up to any rough treatment. Most theatrical costumiers have wig departments, and there are a number of theatrical wigmakers in all the large cities of the world. The fashion for wearing wigs in private life that has persisted for several years makes it easier and cheaper to find suitable wigs.

How to put on wigs, and their basic care

In an opera house one will usually find a wig mistress or wig master who brings the wig to the dressing-room, and puts it on the performer's head. In other branches of the theatre, the wig usually comes in a box, carefully packed in tissue paper, with a ball of tissue inside the wig to keep it in shape. A star usually has his or her wig kept on a wig stand, which is the best thing for the wig. It is essential to pack the wig carefully in its box after every use, and to replace the ball of tissue inside it. A wig that is thrown down on a dressing table will soon look like a bird's nest.

84

Before putting on a wig, women must dispose of their own hair. The most satisfactory way of doing this for short hair is to pin it in circular curls or 'snails' all over the head. This keeps the hair in curl, and provides a smooth correctly shaped head for the wig to cover. Long hair should be divided down the back of the head and wound round the head, the two sides crossing over each other at the back and firmly pinned into place. A firm bandage should then be tied over the hair, either long or short, to keep it in place and act as a base for the wig. An inch and a half or two-inch cotton gauze bandage (bought from any chemist) is best, wound round twice as a turban and firmly knotted or pinned, but some performers prefer a cotton crêpe bandage. For a man wearing a long wig (a shoulder length bob or a restoration periwig) an inch and a half cotton gauze bandage tied moderately tightly round the head and over the ears is often a help in giving a base to which the wig can be pinned.

Wigs have two springs at the nape of the neck, and two in front of the ears. The front of the wig, where it joins the forehead, may have an edging of net, or it may have a forehead piece of gauze. This has a firm straight edge which fits across the forehead, and it must be made up so as to match the face. To put on the wig, lift it in both hands by the springs at the nape of the neck, and hold it so that the centre of the net or forehead piece rests against the centre of your forehead. Pull the wig on with two hands, rather like putting on a bathing cap, until the springs come into place at the nape of the neck. This should bring the front hairline of the wig to roughly where it should lie along the forehead. Always stop pulling just before the hairline reaches the desired position, and then gently ease it back into place. It is not possible to pull a wig forward into place. The wig will not sit, and one is likely to damage its edge. If a wig has come too far back, take it off and start again. Now put your thumbs under the springs at each side of the face, and ease the two side flaps into position, pulling them down as far as they will go. It is generally necessary to fix the flaps (or their net edges) to the face with spirit gum, and it may be necessary to stick the centre of the gauze or net edge of the hairline lightly to the forehead. Press the net on to the area of the spirit gum with a damp cloth, to make it adhere.

With a gauze forehead piece, which pulls straight across the forehead, sticking down is not really necessary, but one must make up the forehead piece lightly to match the face. If one is wearing a Satin Smooth foundation, a light coating of Leichner No. 5 greasepaint will make a good base for it on a new forehead piece. This type of wig can be put on before beginning the make-up and the foundation carried right over the gauze, but it is not advisable to make it up every time that you wear the wig, as this builds up an accumulation of make-up on the forehead piece. If the gauze is painted once a week and powdered each time that it is worn, it should match perfectly, but always check that it has not become discoloured. Nothing looks worse than a forehead that changes colour in a straight line halfway up.

The type of wig with a gauze forehead piece is not used as much nowadays as modern lighting tends to show up the join where the gauze meets the forehead (known as the wig-join). It is still met with in elaborate character wigs, especially those with a receding hairline, where the gauze masks the performer's own hair. With a character, or ageing, make-up, it is possible to camouflage the wig-join by painting a shadow or wrinkle diagonally across it – either the 'V'-shaped shadow suggested in chapter 12, or actual wrinkles, well spaced. There is an admirable example of this in the photograph of Sir Donald Wolfit as Lear (pl 25).

Wigs can be kept close to the face in front of the ears by catching the hair with a very fine hair pin, and sliding the pin under the wig foundation. If a bandage is worn, slide the pin under the bandage, which will hold it even more securely. If the wig is of the wefted type, which is mounted on coarse mesh net, it is possible to pin through the net to secure the wig to the natural hair or the bandage. If the wig is entirely knotted on to gauze, do not pin through it because you will tear the gauze and eventually destroy the wig.

To take off a wig first unstick the net or gauze edging the face, by dabbing the gummed areas with a piece of cotton wool soaked in surgical spirit and then sliding the fingers under the net or gauze to free it. Then take hold of the springs at the nape of the neck with both hands, and pull the wig forward and off. Do not push a wig back off the face, as you are likely to damage the net or gauze edging.

Do not try to dress a wig yourself, even if you are good at hairdressing. Take it back to the wigmaker who supplied it, or to an experienced wig-dresser. Wigs are easily damaged, and expensive to replace. The most that an amateur should attempt with a wig is to comb lightly over the surface to tidy loose hairs (taking care not to comb into the wig, as most wigs are lacquered nowadays), and to replace any small pins that may have shaken out. Anything further calls for a specialist.

Hair pieces
These include switches, falls, curls and chignons for women, and toupées and back pieces for men, and present very few problems. It goes without saying that the hair piece should exactly match the natural hair of the performer. All of the group for women represent long hair, and should be firmly pinned into place with strong hair pins, which should not show. With a fall, which simulates long hair hanging loosely, part the natural hair across the top of the head, from ear to ear, and pin the fall securely to the back hair, with the front edge of the fall coming up against the parting. Then comb the natural front hair back over it, pinning it lightly here and there with very fine hair pins. Make sure that hair pieces are secure before going on to the stage. Nothing is more distracting than a chignon or a bunch of curls slowly sliding off a performer's head, hanging perhaps by one pin, and then lying in a heap on the floor for the rest of the scene.

Toupées are usually lightly fixed with spirit gum, and may have a clip at the back to fix into the natural hair. Unless it is intended to change the shape of the face, make sure that the toupée sits on what was the natural hairline. A toupée worn too far forward can entirely change the character of a face.

Back pieces are sometimes mounted on elastic, and sometimes just pin into position. They represent either a roll of hair on the nape of the neck, or a tie-back (*Tom Jones*). They are becoming rarer because men wear their hair increasingly longer in everyday life. If they are on an elastic, it is essential to part the natural hair along the line on which the elastic will lie across the head, and then comb the front hair back over the elastic so that it does not show at all. The natural back hair should also be combed over the back piece, so that it camouflages the join. If the back piece is fixed into position with hair grips, use the type with a matt surface so that they will not catch the light on the stage. Some hair grips can glitter like diamonds.

Made-up beards, moustaches etc.

Nearly all the false beards, moustaches and side whiskers used on the stage today are of the made-up variety. They are made of real hair knotted into net or gauze and can be bought at any theatrical wigmakers. Like hair pieces, they should match the hair of the performer, although a very slight difference in colour is permissible, as natural beards and moustaches do not always exactly match the owner's hair. They are always stuck on with spirit gum, and very full beards may occasionally have an elastic in addition, which goes over the top of the head. If no wig is being worn, the hair must be parted where the elastic will lie, and then be combed back into position over the elastic to hide it.

Beards, etc., are applied to the finished make-up. Wipe away the foundation over the area that the made-up piece will cover and apply spirit gum to the skin. Allow it to become tacky, and then press the piece firmly into position. Press the edges of the piece firmly to the skin with a damp cloth, to help it adhere. If the beard has a hard edge, which makes too definite a line from a distance, draw a slight shading on to the cheek with a matching eyebrow pencil to look as if the edge of the beard is growing naturally from the face (FIG 44).

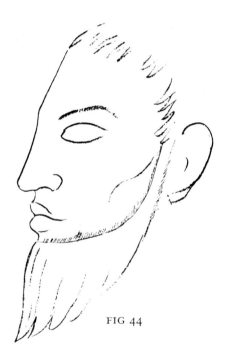

FIG 44

Always check that beards and moustaches reach right up to the natural hairline in front of the ear. Nothing looks more unnatural than a gap of flesh between a beard and the natural hair, or the edge of a wig. If there is a gap, fill it in with light strokes of a matching eyebrow pencil (or greasepaint on a brush) to simulate hair growing on the required area.

When wearing a beard, always make sure that the colour of the neck matches that of the face. Frequently, when a full beard is worn (one that reaches the natural hair line in front of the ears on each side), the performer has a pale old face and a rich, flesh coloured neck, which gives an extraordinarily mask-like effect. Conversely, with a ruddy complexion, a pale neck below the beard will look out of place. The neck and under the chin should always be painted with the same foundation as the face, unless a very high collar is being worn. Even then, it is advisable to powder under the chin with the same coloured powder that was used on the face.

Crêpe Hair

Crêpe hair was once an indispensable part of an actor's equipment, but it is no longer used to any extent. Made-up beards and moustaches have greatly improved in appearance, and also become more easily procurable, and modern lighting shows up the fact that crêpe hair is actually a rather woolly sort of fibre. It is still used occasionally to make a very light curly beard or moustache, to strengthen eyebrows and to make curly side whiskers. A very little of the hair should be used (most performers use far too much), and it should be as near as possible a match to the natural hair – it is obtainable in a wide variety of colours. Wipe the foundation from the area required to be covered by the hair and paint it with spirit gum. While the gum is becoming tacky, tease out a very little of the crêpe hair and press it into position, using as little as possible to obtain the desired effect. *Never* use a solid lump of the hair. For strengthening eyebrows it is not necessary to wipe away the foundation, as this can be messy, and the amount of crêpe hair required is so small that it should adhere with the spirit gum painted on to the finished make-up. A close clipped moustache or beard may be simulated by crêpe hair chopped into very short lengths (about one eighth of an inch) and stuck with spirit gum over the required area.

If one requires a more elaborate beard or moustache made from crêpe hair, it is necessary for the crêpe hair to be straightened. When a large amount is needed (for a beard that is to be worn every night for the run of a play, or for a number of performers in one production) a hank of crêpe hair of the desired colour should be unwound from the two strings that hold it together and soaked in hot water, preferably in a straight-sided jug. When thoroughly wet, the hair is wound tightly round the jug, secured with a hair grip, and left to dry. If only a little is required, tease out a suitable amount and pull it lightly through hot water several times; then press it in a fold of blotting paper until it is dry.

A Vandyke beard can be built up with this straightened hair, applied in sections. Having wiped off the foundation over the area to which the beard is to be secured, paint the area *under* the chin with spirit gum and press a small amount of well-teased out crêpe hair into place, with the hairs pointing straight forward. When they have firmly adhered, trim the projecting hairs to a point, with a pair of scissors. Then paint each side of the chin with spirit gum, and press a smaller amount of hair into place (about half the amount used under the chin) with the hairs running along the line of the jawbone and meeting in a point in front, together with the point of the first (under chin) section. Finally paint the centre of the chin with spirit gum and press another small amount of crêpe hair into place, with hairs running straight up and down. The upper line of the top and side pieces of the beard (where they meet the face) should resemble a 'W'. Finally, trim the finished beard with scissors. If the line where the hair meets the face looks too abrupt, shade it into the face with a matching eyebrow pencil, or with matching greasepaint or lining colour on a brush.

88

A larger beard is made in the same way, with a series of small amounts of crêpe hair along the line of the jawbone as far as is required, if necessary right up to the natural hair line in front of the ears. The normal area for a beard is where the stubble grows on the face, but it can cover a smaller area, as if part of the face has been shaved.

A fairly short moustache is made by painting one half of the upper lip with spirit gum and then sticking one end of a swatch of straightened crêpe hair to the area, with the hairs running downwards from the nose with a slight angle outwards. The crêpe hair is then cut off to the required length, and the process repeated on the other half of the lip. Most short moustaches come out to the end of the mouth, or slightly beyond it. For a larger moustache, stick the hair at a slightly more oblique angle, which will help the outward sweep of the hair.

Whitening the hair

Performers occasionally need to make grey or whiten their own hair for an ageing character, and this can be done in several ways. The classic way, very effective for a slight greying, is to powder the hair with talc, or with powdered starch, which is whiter and is also supposed to act as a dry shampoo. Powdering is only effective when a dull, lifeless look is wanted for the hair, as powdering naturally removes any gloss. Care should be taken to apply the powder either very lightly and evenly all over the hair, or in streaks that run along the length of the hairs. White hair does not occur in powder-puff shaped patches all over the head. Mostly it comes in streaks, above the ears and from the centre of the forehead, from which it spreads. The nape of the neck only goes white when the whole of the rest of the head is white, and not always then. It should always be left the normal colour when the hair is powdered, as the degree of greying achieved by powdering would not, in nature, affect the nape of the neck. Always brush the powder well out of the hair after the performance.

A more natural effect of white streaks can be achieved by using Leichner No. 20 (white) greasepaint, or Max Factor Hair Whitener. They should be applied in light stripes to the hair in appropriate places. The disadvantage of these is that with frequent application they tend to make the hair messy. If strongly marked white stripes are required to be worn for any length of time, it is advisable to have them made on a net edge by a theatrical wigmaker. They can then be stuck on at the hairline, and brushed into the natural hair.

There are hair powders in some colours available to change the colour of the hair. I do not find them very effective, as the result is apt to be patchy, and they take the natural gloss from the hair. It is also possible to buy Hair Lacquers that change the colour of the hair.

17 · Body make-up

The term 'body make-up' covers all areas of the body and limbs apart from the face. We have touched briefly on making-up the hands in previous chapters, but on many occasions large areas of the body have to be made up as well. The most frequent use is in the case of women in nineteenth- or early twentieth-century evening dress, with a great exposure of shoulders and bosom. A healthy suntan may not look out of place with a modern, low-cut dress, but it looks quite wrong with a period costume, as does the pallid grey colour of flesh not accustomed to being exposed. In the early part of this century much use was made of 'wet white' which, as its name suggests, painted the limbs a pearly pink white. It was inclined to brush off on anything with which it came into contact, so that an embrace with a lover in evening dress produced some interesting visual effects. Nowadays Max Factor Pancake is generally used, in a colour one or two shades lighter than the face (faces are nearly always slightly darker than bodies). It should be applied right down to the line of the dress, front and back, and should completely cover the arms and the back of the hands. Apply it as lightly as possible, so as not to get a lacquered effect.

Racial body make-up

In racial make-up – Oriental, Mediterranean, Negro, etc. – any area of the body that is exposed should be related in colour to the face. It need not be an exact match – as we have seen earlier, bodies are usually slightly lighter than faces – but there should be a close tonal and textural resemblance. Leichner and Max Factor both make a variety of body make-up, and of these my favourite is the transparent variety, called Body Tint by Max Factor and Tan Klear by Leichner, who make it in light and dark suntan. Max Factor make five colours – Light Golden Tan (Clear), Medium Golden Tan (264), Dark Tan (265), Red Tan (270) and Dark Olive-Brown (273). I have always found Light Golden Tan (Clear) a good colour for Mediterranean and Middle Eastern make-up, and, applied more heavily, suitable for light skinned Indians and Singalese. Being transparent, these colours can be made darker by using two or more coats of the liquid. This makes Body Tint Clear a good stand-by colour, and it may also be used as a hand make-up which will not rub off. The darker colours can be used as required.

These clear colours are applied with a sponge, taking care to apply them evenly, and not in streaks. They seem pale when they are first applied, but they dry in a few minutes to a darker colour. In cold weather it is advisable to stand the bottle in a bowl of warm water, so that the liquid is body temperature when it is applied. It is not nice to have ice-cold liquid spread over the body.

For really dark colours, Max Factor Pancake is the most suitable. Pancake comes in Negro 1 (light), Negro 2 (dark), Light Egyptian, Dark Egyptian, Light Indian (T.D.4), Dark Indian (665-R), Red Indian (051), Oriental (B.M.), Chinese, Tahitian and Latin (K.F.8), which speak for themselves. These may be applied with water and a sponge. For a dark Negro effect, Negro 2 Pancake applied with Dark Olive Brown (273) Body Tint (as described in the section on Negro make-up in chapter 13) gives the best effect, and has an advantage in that, when it is dry, it can be polished with the palms of the hands to give a sheen to the skin. This greatly adds to the natural look of the make-up. Bear in mind that dark skinned people do not have dark palms to their hands or dark soles to their feet, and when the body make-up is completed, wipe these clean with a damp sponge, or piece of cotton wool.

The opaque liquid body make-up to which we referred earlier also comes in tans and Negro colourings, but I do not find them as suitable for racial effects. They have a tendency to look painted, while the transparent colours look like real skin. For an artificial effect with a stylised or fantastic make-up, or in a revue, one can use Max Factor powder body make-up, sometimes called Texas Earth, which gives a glistening effect, almost as if the body had been powdered with gold over the tan. This comes in Dark Olive Tan (777), Dark Reddish Tan (953) and Dark Copper Tan (282), and is a powder which is applied either dry or with a damp sponge, and is then polished with the hands after it has dried, giving an extra sheen to the skin.

Removing body make-up
All these types of body make-up are easily removed with soap and water, preferably under a shower. In theatres without showers one often sees groups of performers industriously washing the colour off each others' backs.

18 · Summing up of character make-up

In the previous chapters we have ranged over the various forms that make-up can take, and we have considered alternative ways of achieving effects. All of these are only suggestions, based on experience and the basic rules of light and shade. There is no rule of thumb by which a make-up can be achieved, nor is there any 'correct' make-up for any specific character. One must start with the performer's face and then, taking into account the style of the production, the size of the theatre and the type of lighting, one can work toward the effect desired. Because a make-up has been successful on one face, one cannot assume that it will be a success on another. Many of the peculiar make-up effects that one sees are the result of an actor-director imposing his own personal make-up on some unfortunate artist. Equally, a make-up worn successfully by an artist in one production may be completely unsuitable in another, particularly in a different-sized theatre. Many performers wear exactly the same amount of make-up in every theatre, making no allowance for the size of the building. This is apt to make them look over made-up in small theatres and lacking in facial detail in large ones.

To achieve the best results with character make-up, one must ceaselessly observe and experiment. Study the faces that you see in the street and on buses and trains. See how the light catches the folds of the skin, and where the shadows fall. See how a discontented mouth droops, and what exactly causes its expression. Look at the colour and structure of the different racial types, and then experiment with these effects on your own face until you are able to simulate them with a sufficient degree of exaggeration to make them carry to the public. This way you will achieve a make-up that is real and meaningful, and not just an imposed copy of some other person's idea.

Always bear in mind that the hands and any exposed portions of the body must be related to the face in colour and texture. In paler skinned races, as we discussed earlier, the hands and body are generally slightly paler than the face, but in the darker races this difference tends to disappear. Even so, it is always a mistake to paint the face paler than the body, unless a made-up look is required for the face.

In very large theatres, particularly in opera and ballet, bear in mind the extra distance and the intense lighting, and use stronger colours. Draw all the facial details more heavily, but without distorting the shape. Your expression will then carry to the back of the theatre. In smaller theatres, draw everything lightly and softly, and keep the colours closer to nature. By adjusting in this way to the working conditions, your make-up will never look out of place.

List of suppliers

Charles Fox Ltd, 25 Shelton St, London, WC2
Annello & Davide Ltd, 33 Oxford St, London, W1
Wig Creations Ltd, or The Stanley Hall Shop, George St, Baker St, London, W1
Theatre Zoo, New Row, St Martins Lane, London, WC2
W. B. Hubble (Chemist), 41 Cranbourn St, London, WC2
Max Factor Salon, 28 Old Bond St, London, W1X 4BP
Maitland Ltd, 42 Torrington Place, Gower St, London, WC1
The Dancers Shop, 21 Hartfield Crescent, Wimbledon, London
E. C. Maxwell, 6 Lochrim Buildings, Edinburgh
Danswear Centre, 5 Dixon St (off Enoch Square), Glasgow C1
Stage Furnishing, 346 Sauchiehall St, Glasgow C2
Hills Ltd, 1a Bold St, Liverpool
The Sign of Four (Frank Leatherhead), 20 Goldsmith St, Nottingham
Eugene Earle, 16 Cannon St, Preston, Lancs
Royalty Theatrical Agency, 13–15 City Rd, Chester, Cheshire
Brocklehurst, 48 King Edward St, Hull, Yorks
Twinkle Toes, 1 Newcastle House, Barkerend Rd, Bradford, BD3 9AD, Yorks
Watts, 18 New Brown St, Manchester
The Fancy Dress Shop, 260 Old Christchurch Rd, Bournemouth, Hants
Prompt Corner, 7 Carlton Place, Southampton, Hants
The Stage Door, 102 Marmion Rd, Southsea, Hants
Brownes the Chemists, 25 Church St, Leatherhead, Surrey
Mannings Music Shop, 23 St Nicholas St, Ipswich, Suffolk

The Max Factor Salon, 28 Old Bond Street, is always glad to answer queries and keeps a complete stock of theatrical make-up.

The Max Factor Salon, 1655 North McCadden Place, Hollywood, California, is the main salon in U.S.A. and will be glad to supply information concerning their products and main stockists throughout the U.S.A.

The address of the nearest stockist can be obtained from L. Leichner (London) Ltd, Sales Administration Division, 436 Essex Rd, London, N1.

The main wig makers for the theatre in London are:
'Bert', 46 Portnall Rd, W9
Charles Fox Ltd, 184 High Holborn, WC1
Simon (Wigs) Ltd, 2 New Burlington St, W1
Wig Creations Ltd, 25 Portman Close, W1
Wigs may be obtained in the provinces from:
C. & W. May Ltd, Pantomime House, Oozells St, Birmingham 1
William Mutrie & Son Ltd, Proscenium House, Broughton St, Edinburgh 1
W. A. Homburg Ltd, 31 Call Lane, Leeds 1
S. B. Watts & Co, 18-20 New Brown St, Manchester 4 ·

Suppliers in U.S.A.
Max Factor Salon, 1655 North McCadden Place, Hollywood, California
J. Halpern, Co, 810 Penn Avenue, Pittsburg, Pennsylvania
Irving H. Raditz and Co, Berwin, Illinois
Dessart Bros. Inc., Halloween Lane, Department F., West Warwick, Rhode Island

Index